ALSO BY THE AUTHOR

HUNGER
FOR
POWER

WHO RULES THE WORLD

AND

HOW

Andre Bacard

HEROICA BOOKS

SAN RAFAEL, CALIFORNIA

Published by:

Heroica Books
Box 12718-A, Northgate Station
San Rafael, CA 94913, U.S.A.

Library of Congress Cataloging in Publication Data.

Bacard, Andre
    Hunger for power.

    Bibliography: p.
    Includes index.
    1. Power (Social sciences)
    2. Political psychology.
I. Title.
JC330.B23   1986   303.3   85-24794
ISBN 0-935539-10-7
ISBN 0-935539-11-5 (pbk.)

DEDICATION

This book is dedicated, first and foremost, to persons everywhere who prefer freedom to slavery.

I am grateful to Will and Ariel Durant, who delighted me with the power of history; Jean-Paul Sartre and Simone de Beauvoir, who inspired me with the power of intellectual courage; and Bertrand Russell, who enlightened me with the power of skepticism.

In 1983, I founded the Affirmist Society in order to celebrate persons who add to our culture. I am thankful to all members, including our advisors:

Dr. Ray Chasse, Dean at Pacific Western University; Dr. Albert Ellis, Director of the Institute for Rational-Emotive Therapy; Erika Erdmann, author of REALISM AND HUMAN VALUES and research aide for Nobel Laureate Roger Sperry's SCIENCE AND MORAL PRIORITY; Jesse Gordon, President of the Humanist Society of Metropolitan New York; Beatrice Gross, author of THE NEW OLD: STRUGGLING FOR DECENT AGING; Ronald Gross, author of THE INDEPENDENT SCHOLAR'S HANDBOOK; Professor Carl Jensen, Director of Project Censored; Edna Ruth Johnson, Editor of THE CHURCHMAN (founded in 1804); Russ Kingman, author of A PICTORIAL LIFE OF JACK LONDON; Professor

Konstantin Kolenda, author of PHILOSOPHY IN LITERATURE; Professor Gerald Larue, author of SEX AND THE BIBLE; Joe Nickell, author of INQUEST OF THE SHROUD OF TURIN; Professor Richard Paul, Director of the Center for Critical Thinking and Moral Critique; and Robert Rimmer, author of THE HARRAD EXPERIMENT.

Thanks to everyone who responded to my power questionnaire, in particular: Helen Gurley Brown, Editor of COSMOPOLITAN; Professor Noam Chomsky, M.I.T.; Professor Milton Friedman, Nobel Laureate in Economics; Dr. Germaine Greer, author of THE FEMALE EUNUCH; Henry Anatole Grunwald, Editor-in-Chief of TIME, S.I. Hayakawa, former United States Senator; William R. Hewlitt, cofounder of Hewlitt-Packard computer company; Professor Sidney Hook, author of THE HERO IN HISTORY: A STUDY IN LIMITATION AND POSSIBILITY; Lady Bird Johnson, wife of the United States President; William F. Miller, President of SRI; Lloyd Slater, Director of the Academy of Independent Scholars; Dr. Edward Tompkins, scientist; Ted Turner, Chairman of the Board of Turner Broadcasting System; Andrew Young, Mayor of Atlanta and former United States Representative to the U.N.; and Professor Harry Zohn, Brandeis University.

My applause to Genevieve Wilson of Ross, California for her powerful man-tiger illustration.

Special thanks to Dr. Maritza Pick, author of LEAGUE OF LIARS.

The HUNGER FOR POWER has profited from everyone listed above. However, the ideas expressed in this book are my own and do not necessarily reflect the values of those people mentioned above.

TABLE OF CONTENTS

LET US BEGIN....

I
THE POWER TABOO

"In America everybody is of the opinion that he has no social superiors, since all men are equal, but he does not admit that he has no social inferiors, for, from the time of Jefferson onward, the doctrine that all men are equal applies only upwards, not downwards."

—Bertrand Russell

"The men who create power make an indispensable contribution to the nation's greatness. But the men who question power make a contribution just as indispensable.... For they determine whether we use power or power uses us."

—John Fitzgerald Kennedy

People are born to seek power. All that they hold dear, their justice, love, property, and wisdom, are subservient to their epic quest for power. Power is as necessary to the enjoyment of life as water is to the survival of life. Yet a tense silence surrounds this fact. Now that sex can be discussed openly, power remains the last dirty secret. Even the best and brightest persons are squeamish to acknowledge fully their attitudes towards power. This taboo against candor arises from the popular myths that all power is evil, all power is political, and all powerlessness is righteous. The truth is much more affirmative.

Power fascinates persons in all socioeconomic classes, geographical regions, and political parties. Millions of manual laborers, entrepreneurs, and diplomats debate whether United States or Soviet Union politicians are mightier, whether Italian or German soccer players are stronger, and whether Arab shieks or Texas oil barons are wealthier. Competition and comparison intrigue people. It makes people feel potent to rate and to judge other persons, especially other individuals who possess superior talents and resources. People, also, relish gossip about their peers and inferiors. Cafes, homes, and workplaces buzz with lively and colorful rumors about what powers friends, relatives, and employers both possess and lack. People want to know who is ascending and who is descending on the great sociological escalator. Power, be it in the athletic, economic, or social sphere, is at the core of much human discussion.

People devote extraordinary time arguing about power for a compelling, straightforward reason. Namely, power is personal. Every person, regardless of age, education, race, nationality, sex, or social standing, exercises power routinely and is affected by other persons' willful acts. Everyone can change the inanimate world according to a plan, even if his alteration is as commonplace as cooking and eating breakfast. Everyone, including psychotics in straitjackets and prisoners in solitary confinement, can move other living creatures in a specific direction, even if his influence is limited to pesky horseflies. Humans who reside in relative solitude, as did Henry David Thoreau at Walden Pond or John Muir at Yosemite, wield power over themselves and their natural environment. Conversely, everyone is influenced by other humans. A few persons may be peninsulas, but none are islands.

Quantitative power varies enormously from person to person. Instruments of strength may embody children, colleagues, employees, institutions, nations, or the Earth itself. At the top of the scale, 1st century Chinaman Ts'ai Lun invented paper and elevated global civilization. His empowerment added to the wealth of our species. Far lower on the scale, American tycoons require computers in order to keep track of their employees, tenants, and clients. These organizers of wealth own portfolios that fluctuate millions of dollars daily, depending on markets from Hong Kong to Stockholm. A legendary Texan, Bunker Hunt, personifies this superwealth. When testifying before a United States congressional committee about his domination of the world silver market, Hunt announced that a person who knows how much he is worth isn't worth much. Nearer the bottom of the pyramid, illiterate Mexican peasants crawl on their knees to bejeweled churches in order to give thanks for their misery.

Power is a measure of territory. A ghetto housewife in London may dictate the values and behavior of her son. Within the walls of her roach infested cold water flat, she may be a Queen. She may have more motherly authority than Elizabeth II, Queen of England, has over her son Charles, Prince of Wales, at the royal family's country castle. But, at the corner market, the streetsweeper's wife is just one more adult bemoaning the price of milk. If she commands the storekeeper to comb his hair, mother will discover that her empire has limits. Similarly, Ayatollah Khomeni, the fanatical dictator of Iran, has a finite domain. He can command his Islamic devotees to live or die at his whim. But his desire to export his "Holy War" to other countries is meeting strong resistance. Both the housewife and Khomeni are free, they are empowered, to manage the course of events within a well-defined environment. Khomeni's turf is simply the broader of the two.

Qualitative powers are equally diverse. Each of Earth's 5 billion persons is a unique collage of economic, ethical, intellectual, sexual, and social forces of varying competency. One person may be excellent at investing in the stock market, good at solving mathematical puzzles, mediocre at keeping promises, poor at making love, and terrible at selecting spouses. A second person might be an empowered lover and an impotent investor. These specific qualities of power, these talents, define and differentiate both individuals. Furthermore, each person oscillates frequently between positions of relative ability and debility.

Power reflects environment. A person's power at a specific spacetime depends upon both his or her talents and upon nearby persons' priorities. Arnold Schwarzenegger, the world champion bodybuilder, would be the unquestionable center of focus on a French Riviera beach. His Herculean physique would polarize women into two groups: those intimidated by his huge muscles and those magnetized by his animal energy. For the latter women, the Austrian-born weightlifter would embody social and sexual power. Richard L. Garwin, a normal sized person, would receive less adoration on the Mediterranean shoreline. However, at an American Association for the Advancement of Sciences convention, Mr. Schwartznegger would play a less powerful role. His excellences would be judged irrelevant, if not silly, by the crowds of sedentary biologists, chemists, and physicists. The spotlight would shift to Garwin, who engineered the first hydrogen bomb in 1952. Garwin's talk about "The Arms Race and Defense Contractors" would touch upon social, economic, and political powers.

Human beings want to enlarge their territory and shape their environment. This is the essence of the power urge. An ambitious San Francisco computer entrepreneur will grow dissatisfied with California markets and start crossing statelines. In addition, as his wealth and goals rise, he may race Ferraris to seduce women, play racquetball to court judges, and sponsor charities to titillate society columnists. His upward mobility is limited only by his imagination and resourcefulness. On a grander scale, Napoleon Bonaparte extended his territory from the school yard, where he directed snowball fights, to Europe's meadows, where he commanded armies. But to govern Europe's men and soil was insufficient reward or challenge for the Emperor. The Corsican wanted to stamp his tastes on culture. He did so, as historian Will Durant noted, by promoting Italian operas with their melodious arias and dramatic plots; by patronizing classical painters with their order and restraint; and by pushing Pierre Corneille's plays with their exultation of heroism and nobility.

People, except for a small and sluggish minority, are unsatisfied conquerers who seek new frontiers. Unlike other animals, their desires are boundless and incapable of total satisfaction. They want more from their decades on this planet than the clothes on their back, the food in their cupboard, and the roof over their head. They are HOMO SAPIENS ("wise ones") and want to prevail, not just to endure. The most conscious and frank persons desire to become gods or, if less driven, to chose their gods. The most celebrated individuals, the Mohandas Gandhis and Martin Luther Kings among us, have been welcomed as demigods by millions of ecstatic persons. Followers have basked in the glory of these leaders' victories. These two seminal figures, as did many persons whose names have been forgotten, wanted to persuade one more person to their viewpoint and sought to climb one step higher.

The epic journey towards power often generates bad

feelings. A woman who sacrificies a decade of family vacations in order to campaign for the United States Senate is likely to be disappointed when, once elected, she arrives in Washington. On Capitol Hill, she will discover that deeply entrenched lobbyists, bureaucrats, and fellow legislators undermine her election promises and ideals. It may shock her to discover that paperwork outweighs glory. If the legislator is myopic, she will fall into an emotional trap. She will resent her impotence, the gap between what her nation is and what she wishes it to be, and she will forget her potency, the gulf between her present position and her farmgirl childhood. This murky state can lead her to utter something misleading, such as: ''Power is an illusion. It isn't what it appears to be.''

Many superstitionists contribute to the power taboo. They beg idols, kiss lucky charms, and read astrology charts because these activities are less taxing than to emulate heroes, embrace hard work, and study astronomy. Their laziness puts them at the mercy of a Cosmos that does not care whether they live or die. A series of inevitable failures follows. Soon, these wounded persons began to echo a battle cry: ''Power corrupts, and absolute power corrupts absolutely.'' They preach that powerlessness, which is to say their lack of effectiveness, is righteous. They want us to believe that being a Jew in the Soviet Union, a black in South Africa, or an illiterate in the United States is ''spiritually'' preferable to being the master of one's destiny! From the other side of their mouth, these advocates of irrational martyrdom complain that their employers receive more benefits and status than themselves.

Beware of such naysayers. It can cost you dearly to interpret their rhetoric literally. In practice, these persons crave power. They are simply too slothful to work for it openly. Their power urge is disguised as love of ease, love of pleasure, love of approval, and love of submission. Towards these goals, they pursue hosts whom they can live off parasitically. The hypochondriac, who fabricates ailments in order to be served breakfast in bed, and the wayward child, who decries life's injustices in order to be included in his parents' wills, are two commonplace manipulators. These persons make a virtue of weakness because that is their road to power. "Blessed are the meek, for they shall inherit the earth" is a war cry of persons who seek ultimate triumph.

Mass media reinforce the power taboo. Television reporters, for example, labor under fierce pressure to manufacture "news" that can be broadcast in thirty second segments. They treat the who, why, and where of world events superficially at best. There is no time for them to analyse their stories in depth, because tomorrow brings another deadline. This frantic pace convinces the public that powerful persons are "overnight successes," that a few leaders mysteriously appear out of nowhere, like winning lottery tickets. The process of power is either ignored or farcified.

The print media is, on the whole, better than television. Even so, it focuses upon the ephemeral and trivial. A daily newspaper recently published a series of editorials about San Francisco's mayor, Diane Feinstein. The editors wrote about Feinstein's debate with the city council about taxation for a new sewer project. These columns were redigested by Bay Area opinion makers. Anyone listening to television news or to radio talk shows heard citizens decry that San Francisco's fate depended on the outcome of this Great Debate. Feinstein was portrayed as the embodiment of power. By comparison, the same news gatherers barely mentioned the development of a new telescope by Charles Townes, the University of California physicist credited with inventing the revolutionary laser. Townes' latest tool, which may profoundly affect our species, was given second billing to the gutter.

On a graver scale, society provides enormous publicity for the likes of Adolf Hitler. We publish books, produce movies, and replay documentaries about the demonic German. Gregory Pincus, by comparison, is a media unknown. Pincus, the American biologist who led the invention of the oral contraceptive pill, has altered the ethics, behavior, and bodies of billions of men, women, and children from the largest cities to the tiniest villages. All over the Earth, his pill has reduced starvation and impoverishment due to overpopulation. He has helped cultures of every color, race, and creed. However, most molders of public opinion are unimpressed by Pincus' humanitarianism. They judge Pincus, the hero, less powerful than Hitler, the antihero.

Many historians and social pundits fare little better than yellow journalists. The formers' emotions and intellects are tied in knots by the power taboo. They write or teach about the powerful, but resent any real signs of power in their colleagues or students. Let us be frank. These critics have little power themselves and, not surprisingly, dislike those who do. These equivocal social commentators tend to sympathize with Horace Walpole's words to William Mason in 1778: "What a dreadful thing it is for such a wicked little imp as man to have absolute power!" All affirmative persons should rise above this thinly veiled misanthropy.

Power is an emotionally charged concept. When we

exercise power, we boast and call it "influence." However, when someone else employs power, we imagine selfish and sinister plots. Our double standard is similar to sexual hypocrisy. In Victorian England (and not so much has changed), it was strictly taboo for decent folk to admit that they enjoyed sex. In modern society, it is unfashionable for ethical persons to talk about the almost universal hunger for power. Even Machiavellians pay lip service to the power taboo. We hear the Kremlin elite, who have private traffic lanes on Moscow streets, proclaim that the Soviet Union has no ruling class. We remember President Lyndon Johnson, who fought tooth and nail his entire life for special privileges, state in his modest Texas drawl, "Power? The only power I've got is nuclear and I can't use it." These confessions point to a useful truth. Namely, power is best understood with a generous sprinkling of humor and irony.

The purpose of this book is twofold: first, to describe power's affirmative role and, secondly, to empower you. We assume that you are a dynamic participant in our ongoing dialogue and not a passive onlooker. The next eight chapters examine power in relation to your tastes and appetites, your leaders and followers, your fears about death, your sense of fairplay, and your successes and failures. The final chapter discusses the practical dynamics of attaining power. Some of you will profit most by beginning with chapter nine.

At each juncture, I will demonstrate beyond a reasonable doubt that the greatest powers benefit humankind, that the most enduring powers are apolitical, and that habitual powerlessness is disastrous. I shall contend that it is more rational to face helplessness directly, and to do something about it, than to hide behind innocence, ignorance, or hypocrisy.

My inspiration for this project stems, first, from the exhiliratingly potent and depressingly impotent persons whom I have known and, secondly, from my study of history and science. One goal of this book is to continue where Nietzsche's WILL TO POWER and Bertrand Russell's POWER left off and to offer a fresh alternative to Machiavelli's THE PRINCE.

II
THE HUNGER FOR POWER

"Hunger and love are what move the world."

—Johann Schiller

"Let me have men about me that are fat,
Sleek-headed men and such as sleep o'nights.
Yond Cassius has a lean and hungry look,
He thinks too much; such men are dangerous."

—Shakespeare's Julius Caesar

"God Himself dare not appear to a hungry man except in
the form of bread."

—Mahatma Gandhi

Human hunger for power begins at birth. When Sigmund Freud emerged from the warm security of his mother's womb and his umbilical cord was cut, he was a helpless, naked animal. A human baby cannot, as can a newborn alligator, swim into a nearby pool of water, open its mouth, and grab a minnow for its first meal. Rather, Freud was totally dependent upon adult humans. When hunger pains gnawed at him, the Freiberg baby did the best he could. He cried for attention and hoped that someone would respond. He did not ask for pudding, cereal, or bananas. These foodstuffs were unknown to him and, besides, the future writer had no vocabulary. He pleaded for a person who could select, gather, and prepare food for him. The baby who would someday found psychoanalysis reached out for the ability to organize the world in his behalf. Freud, as do all babies, called out for power!

This intimate bond between the hunger to be fed and the power to feed is lifelong. Nonetheless, the tie between the pain of hunger and the joy of power is often knotted with mystery. It is time to unravel the "power hungry" process that enabled Freud to write THE INTERPRETA-TION OF DREAMS and that permits so many people to survive.

Hunger, in its simplest form, is a physiological process. When Freud put food into his mouth, a series of biochemical reactions began. The Austrian physician's tongue, with its taste buds, sensed sweet, sour, salt, and bitter. Glands on each side of his jaw secreted saliva that emulsified the food and made it easier to swallow. Next, a nearly colorless stomach juice consisting mainly of hydrochloric acid and three enzymes (rennin, pepsin, and lipase) began breaking down the Jewish scientist's lunch into usable chemicals. The intestines carried out the bulk of his digesting and absorbing. When there was no food in Freud's thirty foot alimentary canal that extended from his mouth to his rectum, trouble began. His stomach muscles began wavelike muscular contractions which, in turn, irritated his stomach's nerve endings. This involuntary process sent signals to the private practitioner's brain, which interpreted the stimulation as pain and told Freud that it was time to eat. By and large, Freud possessed the socioeconomic and personal resources to respond appropriately to his body's survival message.

A primordial power is the ability to secure food. Wellfed humans are more likely to become life-affirming entrepreneurs, inventors, or scientists than their starving neighbors. Tragically, countless individuals are impotent to satisfy biological hunger. Three meals a day is a luxury. For half of our species, a second or third daily meal is an impossible dream. More than 1,000,000,000 people live with fear of famine. The brightest, most industrious of these persons lack sufficient water, tools, and fertile soil to cultivate the food that their bodies crave. They are forced to ingest poorly balanced diets of rice, beans, and bread or, worse yet, to compete with wild animals for insects, roots, and tree leaves. For these persons, whom Franz Fanon called the "wretched of the earth," terrorism and revolution are much more appealing than psychoanalysis. Biological hunger coupled with the inability to eat properly is a time bomb waiting to explode.

Many affluent people suffer a more subtle, but equally dangerous, impotence. These persons, out of ignorance or laziness, reply poorly to biological hunger. The United States harvests an enormous surplus of eatable animals and plants. Even so, millions of Americans who can afford nutritious food are malnourished. They ingest harmful quantities of alcohol, tobacco, drugs, and other substances that make them listless, unable to concentrate, and abnormally susceptible to infection. Sometimes, these self-destructive chemical habits cause terrible pain. Jack Kerouac, the great novelist, drank himself to death. Back in Europe, Freud inhaled so many hot, toxic gases (tobacco smoke) that he contracted jaw cancer and required thirty operations on his mouth.

The gnaw of hunger is, clearly, more than just abdominal discomfort. Kerouac and Freud fed a different sort of hunger. Appetite, even in the clinical medical sense, is more complex than the contraction of muscles. Hospital patients who have undergone a gastrectomy, who have had their stomach removed by surgery, still feel hunger. At first, this fact sounds remarkable. So does researchers' suggestion that hunger can be generated by decreased glucose in the blood stream. But, on second thought, there is little cause for surprise. Hunger is evoked by dreaming about a banquet, by remembering a delicious smell, or by hearing an alarm clock. Hunger reflects our attitudes, our tastes, about life.

Tastebuds are, to speak metaphorically, a dynamic relation between an individual and his environment. Our tastes reflect our powers. Alfred Adler, one of Freud's colleagues, may have enjoyed applesauce and milk from his earliest Viennese meals until his last supper. We have no way of knowing. In either case, the founder of Individual Psychology certainly evolved out of childhood and embraced a richer universe in adulthood. The author of ORGAN INFERIORITY AND ITS PSYCHICAL COMPENSATION deepened and broadened his tastes. His personal growth had biological and cultural origins. As an infant, Adler lacked the sharp teeth and strong jaws to chew beef steak and the dexterity to shell peanuts. Greater muscular power and agility in adulthood allowed him to prefer or reject these foods based on tastes, rather than practical concerns. Culturally, Adler wrote influential books. These works enabled him to lecture worldwide and to be appointed America's first professor of medical psychology (now called psychiatry) at Long Island Medical School. Travel and career opportunities permitted Adler to savor what was beyond his childhood grasp.

Biological hunger evolves into psychological and socioeconomic hungers quite naturally. Once children are able to feed themselves, they use forks, knives, and spoons. Some of these utensils are plastic; others are silver. Each instrument has its own touch. Each eating tool has its separate social and economic cost. Children discriminate. They favor one type of fork more than another. Also, they learn to discern between wooden plates and fine china. They rank these eating platters. Children who highly prefer the aesthetics of silver and porcelain are likely to develop greater monetary hungers than children who enjoy the practicality of plastic and wood.

Food is at the core of human socialization. Most animals feed; but most humans eat. Unlike tigers, human diners have elaborate rules. For us, gorging is frowned upon. So is eating live or bloody meat. I suspect that Freud and Adler learned to use spoons, not their hands, and to organize their dinner, rather than to stir beets and ice cream into one mound. They gathered to drink ale and sherry from distinct glasses. This social adaptation literally opens the door to new worlds. From the spoon in childrens' mouths, to the stove in their kitchens, to their local grocery stores, biological hunger exposes children to ever enlarging circles of social challenges.

Healthy persons exit childhood's kitchen door and enter adulthood's living room with diverse wants. If they reside in cultures that permit escape from abject poverty, they will long for consumer items that are more expensive and less essential than kitchenwares. If their humanity is deeper, they will strive for more substantial goals than automobiles and televisions. Philosopher and civil libertarian Corliss Lamont wrote that the social good firmly entails such values as health, significant work, economic security, friendship, sex love, community recognition, educational opportunity, a developed intelligence, freedom of speech, cultural enjoyment, a sense of beauty, and opportunity for recreation. These twelve

25

major affirmations are important derivatives of biological hunger.

Hunger, in this broader sense, is an individual's desire or craving to achieve a goal. This definition of hunger causes us to stop and reflect. Power is the ability to bring about an intended effect, the capacity to attain a specific end. Hunger and power, therefore, are inseparable social and biological realities. Hunger is the emotional drive behind power. Hunger urges a person to apply labor, resources, and talent towards the actualization of his dreams. The object, goal, dream, or end that a person seeks may be to eat a ham sandwich, to fly an airplane, or to comprehend Shakespeare's JULIUS CAESAR. Whatever a person's ambition might be, however mundane or lofty, it is certainly not bestowed upon him by birth. Genes provide a person with the instinct to survive, but environment provides the individual with a detailed outline of how to prosper. And, as William Faulkner noted in his Nobel Prize acceptance speech, mankind's goal is not only to endure, but to prevail.

Biochemical hunger requires neither a vivid imagination, a sharp intelligence, nor a strong will. For this reason, it evokes less controversy than does sociological hunger. One of my lectures, ''The Virtues of Power,'' infuriated one of the authors who was present. He kept insisting, over glasses of brandy, ''All power corrupts and absolute power corrupts absolutely.'' In that man's eyes, all powerful persons are greedy and insatiable. As I listened to the obese gentleman, I watched him eat a series of chocolate pastries buried in whipped cream. This is not the place to analyse the sociologist's craving for sweets, nor to imagine his confessions. But it is safe to guess that this detestor of avarice consumed more than his share of calories for reasons unrelated to an empty stomach. Newspapers do not condemn gluttonous persons for being "food hungry" and selfish with the same enthusiasm that they brand financial connoisseurs "power hungry" and covetous. In this matter, humor is welcome. Some hungers are easier and, therefore, more fashionable than others.

Hunger, the impulse away from deprivation towards fulfillment, occurs in various degrees. It is most intense when the gap between who a person is and who he believes he can become is greatest. In 1932, Richard Kleberg of Texas' famous King Ranch empire, ran for election to the United States Congress against a San Antonio businessman named Thurman Barrett. This battle sparked a relatively unknown schoolteacher to quit his job and join the Kleberg campaign. When Kleberg won the election and moved to Washington, that precocious teacher named Lyndon Baines Johnson became his secretary. I have a hunch that the future President Johnson had an extraordinary hunger in those years. Johnson was dissatisfied with his status quo and wanted personal progress.

Nietzsche, in his THE WILL TO POWER, understood the hunger of persons like Johnson. The German philosopher noted that the normal dissatisfaction of our drives, for example, hunger and the sexual drive, should not be viewed as depressing. Dissatisfaction, instead of making one disgusted with life, should provide a great stimulus to life.

In 1934 in Winsted, Connecticut, a woman gave birth to a baby who now personifies the fusion of biological and sociological hunger. This youngest child's Lebanese parents operated a restaurant and a bakery. The boy's father, with the zeal of an Old Testament prophet, thundered over the dinner table about justice much the way Joseph Kennedy preached to his children about power. The youngster was moved deeply by his father's passion for ethics. While still too young to attend school, the disciplined boy began sitting at the local courthouse and listening to lawyers argue their cases. By adolescence, he had read great muckraking books such as Upton Sinclair's THE JUNGLE, as well as accounts about Alexander the Great and Genghis Khan's conquests. Among his favorite novels were Zane Grey's western adventures. This boy, Ralph Nader, had the burning inner core required of all heroic Davids who best Goliaths.

Nader was reared in the same consumer society as millions of other persons. But he hungered, he starved, to improve our culture. Towards that end, he excelled academically and graduated from Harvard Law School. His first great triumph was to investigate a sacred cow, the Detroit automobile industry, and to publish UNSAFE AT ANY SPEED. This book, which catapulted him to national prominence in 1965, cried out for safer cars under Nader's conviction that the United States Constitution nowhere declares the duty of citizens to fly through windshields (due to no seatbelts). Subsequent battles by Nader led Congress to pass the Wholesome Meat Act of 1967, requiring inspection of meat packing houses for sanitary conditions; the Federal Coal Mine Health and Safety Act of 1968, correcting dangers of working in mines; the Radiation Control for Health and Safety Act of 1968, reducing exposure to unnecessary radiation; and the Consumer Product Safety Act, addressing a broad range of consumer issues. In a seven year period, ending in 1973, Congress passed more than twenty-five consumer and environmental laws largely due to the tireless efforts of Nader. The hungry man also contributed to passage of a law not found in any other country, the Freedom of Information Act of 1974. This legislation allowed citizens to examine government records to check if laws were being enforced.

"How many of you are hungry to become fighters for justice in America?" is a common opening line in Ralph Nader's speeches. The hunger that he speaks of is a passion to establish a fifth estate to represent the public against what Nader sees as an unholy alliance between corporations and government regulators. The estate, which stands on the shoulders of William Jennings Bryan and 19th century populists, Teddy Roosevelt and the turn of the century muckrakers, and Senators Estes Kefauver and Hubert Humphrey, is directed towards many causes, as the legislation in the last paragraph indicates.

Nader, though he can laugh at himself, is a fanatic about food. Journalist Ken Auletta reports that lean and hungry Nader claims to eat only fourteen pounds of meat per year, questions whether grape juice is really made of grapes, and believes cigarette smokers are weak in character. Nader gets mad, according to press reports, when photographers try to snap his picture while he is eating. These anecdotes all come together in one concise statement by the empowered warrior whose actions point towards nothing less than the qualitative reform of the Industrial Revolution. Regarding his notoriety, Nader is reported to have said, "I could have gone to Hollywood and married a starlet and gotten fat and talked about what I used to do."

The abnormal hunger that accompanies all substantial achievement confuses and intimidates many persons of average appetite. These persons applaud the boxing skills of Muhammed Ali, the environmental victories of Rachel Carson, and the consumer safeguards of Ralph Nader but, simultaneously, view these leaders with suspicion. It is commonly believed that anyone who willingly forfeits picnics, vacations, and football games in order to work must be emotionally off balance. Harsher critics of success try to debunk eminence by nitpicking. I have heard people belittle the nonviolence of Gandhi on the grounds that he, as an elderly man, took virgins to bed without engaging in sex. Actually, these attacks point out the need of weak persons to believe that powerful acts are illusions, but that lesser achievements are not!

Exceptional hunger should be cherished. It is the noble drive that makes total commitment possible. All athletes feel the physiological and emotional high that accompanies an hour of jogging, swimming, or lifting weights. During such a workout, time appears to stop. The exerciser feels immortal, and his senses explode with vitality. The entrepreneur, musician, or philosopher who labors sixteen hours a day and seven days a week is familiar with the same magic. His work is not a sacrifice. Rather, it is a great pleasure. When the creator strolls on the beach, every grain of sand and cry of gulls kindles his inner fire and reminds him that life, without his all absorbing business, symphony, or book, would be a sound and fury signifying nothing. The ballet choreographer who suddenly realizes that she has not slept in two days because of her love of ''Swan Lake,'' should not be pitied or scorned. She should be recognized and emulated. For she is one of the luckiest human beings on Earth. Her power to influence culture, her fame to attract the best dancers, and her money to travel are a result of, not the cause of, her inner hunger, her passion for life.

Hunger, unless accompanied by appropriate talent, turns to the jaws of corruption. The small minority of journalists who plagiarize in order to earn a Pulitzer Prize, the businessmen who embezzle from their partners in order to purchase a Rolls Royce, and the athletes who mortgage their bodies with drugs in order to win an Olympic medal have bitten off greater ambition than they can digest honestly. They are flawed not by high goals, but by low abilities. This shortcoming drives people to lie, steal, and swindle. In plush Wall Street offices, anxious stock manipulators bilk investors for millions of dollars whereas, in filthy ghetto alleys, their counterparts knife laborers for cab fare. Both groups of persons are intrinsically weak. We agree with Adler that they are cowards. They believe that to cheat, "to beat the system," is the quickest and easiest way to satisfy their hunger. Whether or not such people are caught and punished, they are wrong.

Public discredit of individuals in high places tantalizes many unempowered people who secretly long for greater power. Richard Nixon was driven from the White House in disgrace because of the Watergate Scandal. But political commentators erroneously blamed Nixon's Waterloo on his excessive power hunger. The President's problem was not his hunger, but his weakness. Nixon knew good and well that a team of men working for his re-election committee had broken into the Democratic party's campaign headquarters in Washington. He, also, realized that political espionage is common practice throughout the world and has been for thousands of years. Nixon lacked the courage to admit these facts to the American people and to prosecute the burglars. He was too common a man to set an example of better government.

Rather, the Whittier, California version of Machiavelli tried to cover up the involvement of his colleagues and friends in the pathetic name of "national security" (translated "Nixon's security"). Mr. Nixon's crime was his cynical and pathological disregard for unpleasant truths. Just as a person can choke to death on broiled salmon, by lacking the good sense to distinguish bones from flesh, Nixon lacked table manners.

The impulse towards corruption seduces groups, not only individuals. A few highly vocal Christian evangelists tell us that men, women, and children are evil, but that large corporations, churches, and other organizations are not. These apologists for authority and conformity are wrong. Tens of overpopulated, undereducated, and malnourished nations are highly influenced by American movies and news agencies. Many people in these countries believe that the United States is full of millionaires with oil wells in their backyards, gorgeous women with satin sheets in public bedrooms, and recently arrived immigrants with servants in their kitchens. Not surprisingly, these consumers of mass media develop a hunger for the "good life." They develop anxiety, what the Danish philosopher Kierkegaard called the difference between reality and potentiality. However, residing in underdeveloped economies and in socially rigid cultures, they are powerless to touch the forbidden fruit that is flaunted before them. Frustration builds and leads to hatred of America. Too often, this irrational tension feeds armies, political machines, and terrorist organizations that seek the an age old "short-cut" to opportunity by extorting, kidnapping, and murdering those with whom they wish to exchange places.

Corruption is self-destructive. Nixon pushed himself

and the United States into years of malaise that, with a
little integrity, could easily have been avoided.
Sometimes, corruption is harder to see. More than thirty years ago, a relatively unknown physician published an
article in a scholarly journal. He reported that he had been
able to form antibodies that effectively destroyed three
dreaded types of polio viruses. This news was broadcast
throughout the world, and Jonas Salk became a household
word. Within the next six years, his Salk vaccine helped
prevent about three hundred thousand cases of polio in the
United States. But not all was rosy for Dr. Salk. His vast
publicity rubbed his fellow doctors the wrong way. He was
not invited to join the National Academy of Sciences and
found critics at every turn. Salk was reminded that his
vaccine was mere "applied science," that the real credit
belonged to Havard doctors Enders, Weller, and Robbins,
who had demonstrated that polio viruses could be grown
in specific tissue cultures of primate cells. They, not Salk,
were awarded the Nobel Prize. Salk, for all his courage and
talent in aiding humanity, found jobs closed to him. "The
worst tragedy that could have befallen me was my success," he said later. "I knew right away that I was through,
cast out." In 1963 he founded the Salk Institute for
Biological Sciences in La Jolla, California and observed,
"I couldn't possibly have become a member of this institute if I hadn't founded it myself." The American
medical profession, by treating Salk so poorly, corrupted
its public image.

The hunger for power involves many ironies. In particular, persons have difficulty seeing themselves in
others. I remember a recent luncheon. "What a power
hungry man!" exclaimed a grey haired and impeccably
attired businessman who was sitting across the table from

me. From our window table at one of San Francisco's elegant restaurants, the man in his fifties stared intently at President Ronald Reagan's approaching limousine. His jaw tightened. "A man's gotta be mighty insecure to drive himself as hard as Reagan. He always needs the spotlight," he announced bitterly.

Reagan's black Cadillac, flanked by an entourage of motorcycle policemen and followed by local politicians, glided silently and methodically through the steets of Bagdad by the Bay. Bordering the flashing red lights of police authority, thousands of pedestrians pressed against the granite walls and showcase windows of hotels and department stores. A few people cheered; many booed; and the majority stood silently as the fleet approached their spot on Union Square. But all of the onlookers, the executives, clerks, tourists, and vagrants, had something in common. Namely, they chose to stand shoulder to shoulder on a cold, windy sidewalk in order to glimpse at a man who eats breakfast in the White House. They wanted, if only for a few seconds, to share the power, the glory, and the mythology of another human. Whether they admired or scorned Reagan was irrelevant.

My companion was a Democrat opposed to Reagan, who judged the politician too selfish. Here was a gutsy, acclaimed entrepreneur who had squashed business competitors, sacrificied his wife and children, and driven himself to a heart attack in order to climb out of the poverty of his Tennessee childhood. He was condemning a Hollywood actor with less than one tenth of his wealth for being inordinately driven. Only weeks before, I had visited the mogul's thousand acre estate in northern California. There, surrounded by his vineyard, his race horses, and his private landing strip complete with Lear jet, we discussed the Reagan administration's paranoia about the tiny nation of Cuba. With obvious pride, my host confided to me, "Hell, Fidel Castro isn't a communist. He's a dictator just like me!"

People tend to hunger for other persons' privileges, while ignoring others' trials and tribulations. This is equally true of tyrants and servants. To become President, an individual must undertake an enormously tiring campaign that lasts for years. He must flatter financial patrons whom he personally detests, travel in behalf of party candidates who have opposed him for years, attend conferences with excruciatingly boring bureaucrats, repeat the same speech thousands of times, and eat every overcooked meal put on his plate. This painstaking and often humiliating path to the White House requires both an enormous hunger and an iron stomach. It is little wonder that only a dozen persons out of the 100,000,000 elgible adults in America apply for the job.

In summary, hunger begins as a biological need to move beyond present pain and towards future pleasure. This process of satisfying ourselves permits us to survive. But hunger, the emotive force behind the will to power, can be satisfied only in the short-term. Digestion and elimination of waste follows. Therefore, hunger is never fully satisfied. We always want more. To strive for new food, new challenges, is part of human nobility. Additional nourishment permits our cells to grow, our civilization to advance, and us to affirm life.

III
LEADERS AND FOLLOWERS

"All the world's a stage, and all the men and women merely players. They have their exits and their entrances; and one man in his time plays many parts."
—Shakespeare

"And when we think we lead, we are most led."
—Lord Byron

The hunger for power has two complementary, equally intense impulses: the passion to lead and the desire to
follow. The dualities of employer and employee, prophet
and devotee, and teacher and student embody the two
sides of the power urge. In this chapter, we shall explore
the dynamic interaction between leaders and followers.

Human inequality is a historical fact. C.L. Woolley,
author of THE SUMERIANS, tells us that the Sumerian
civilization of six thousand years ago had stratified social
classes. Gold ornaments and silver jewelry were found in
a few of their tombs. Whoever owned these precious
metals undoubtedly legislated social behavior, just as
owners of diamond mines write the rules in present day
South Africa. Over the millennia, enormous social
upheavals and seemingly irreversible changes have occurred. But, just as a gyroscope returns to equilibrium, social
inequality remains essentially the same. The elite may be

called chiefs, priests, or presidents. The unchosen may be named slaves, serfs, or proletariat. The faces and titles have differed throughout the ages but not the ageless need for hierarchy.

The ratio between the number of leaders and followers is debatable. George Bernard Shaw, the Irish dramatist, once asked Henry M. Stanley, the journalist who explored the unchartered Congo River, how many men could lead his expedition if Stanley became ill. Stanley responded quickly, "One in twenty." During the Korean War, the Chinese discovered that, when they placed the dominant five per cent of their American captives in a separate prison, the remaining ninety-five percent made no attempt to escape. Historian Will Durant states, in THE LESSONS OF HISTORY, "If we knew our fellow men thoroughly we could select thirty percent of them whose combined ability would equal that of all the rest. Life and history do precisely that..." Whether we consider 5% or 30% of the population as leaders, dominant persons are in the minority.

Leaders and followers regularly change roles. Suppose that 5% of America's 240,000,000 citizens are qualified and motivated to lead others. Clearly, 12,000,000 individuals cannot become national leaders. The bulk of these natural supervisors must exercise lesser leadership. They become parents, teachers, or coaches. At their home, school, and baseball league they direct children, students, and athletes. But, elsewhere in society, they defer to police officers, nuclear physicists, and visual artists. In one environment, citizens are leaders; in the next, followers. Therefore, when we speak of leaders, we mean persons who direct most situations that they encounter.

To classify persons as primarily leaders or followers

is not to pass an ethical judgment. Vladimir Zworykin, the inventor of the television camera, was brilliant. But many leaders are cerebral midgets. John F. Kennedy, the former American president, was a scintillating orator. But some leaders are tongue-tied. Duke Ellington, the supreme jazz talent, gave joy to millions of persons through his music. But countless other leaders destroy culture through their prejudices. Followers also come in all varieties. They can be decent citizens or scoundrels. Thus, when we speak of leaders and followers, we are merely acknowledging social roles.

Leaders and followers will always coexist. Generals and soldiers, composers and music fans, inventors and consumers need one another. The good news is that, sometimes, leaders and followers realize their mutual indebtedness. The bad news is that, at other times, society's diverse members ignore their common destiny.

Let us begin by exploring the enjoyable facts of life. Four bonds pull leaders and followers closer together: the centralization of information, the specialization of labor, the pursuit of glory, and the safety of conformity.

The first bond between leaders and followers is the centralization of information. People need accurate facts in order to make intelligent decisions. Take the capitalist stock market, for example. Until recently, many financial brokers lacked sufficient facts. The government securities that they bought and sold changed costs hourly, but traders had to rely upon daily newspapers and telephone calls for recent quotes. This inefficient system ended when Neil Hirsch invented the Telerate system. Hirsch computerized data about the world's money markets, so that buyers and sellers from Hong Kong to New York could assess up to the minute financial news with the push of a button. Hirsch created an information network with him at the center. This established him as a leader for more than fourteen thousand clients, or followers.

Information is power. Many contemporary entrepreneurs, sociologists, and journalists realize this. They forecast that the 21st century will greet an Information Age that will replace our Industrial Age. This "new" culture will be ruled by those individuals who control computers, space stations, and mass media. This scenario is exciting, but not unique. In feudal China, whoever guarded tax records and state secrets governed society. These Chinese simply used finger operated abaci and bamboo sheets, rather than digital computers and microfilms, to tabulate accounts and to transmit coded messages. Then, as always, leadership roles in every field of endeavor tend to go to the few knowledgeable individuals.

The unequal distribution of information creates two classes: teachers and students. You have witnessed these groups interchange knowledge in academic schools, dance studios, or martial arts institutes. These social organizations enable teachers to earn a living by leading students to build a better life. Each class empowers the other.

Teachers and students come together to apply information towards compatible goals. In 1951, Margaret Sanger, who first coined the phrase "birth control," and Katherine McCormick, heiress to the International Harvester farm machinery fortune, taught that women deserved greater freedom. These leaders knew little about medicine, but they had a dream. They approached Gregory Pincus, a student of mammalian reproduction, and asked if he could invent and manufacture a safe, inexpensive contraceptive that women could swallow. Pincus said that he would need a laboratory and assistants to find out. McCormick jumped at the opportunity. "Look here. I'm close to eighty and I want it done in my life time," she said. She wrote Pincus a check for forty thousand dollars as a downpayment on more than two million dollars that she would ultimately give the biologist. Within that decade, Sanger's, McCormick's, and Pincus' goal was fulfilled. The birth control pill became a reality.

Teachers can improve life for all followers. In 1900, Karl Landsteiner discovered human blood types. He transformed the once rare and dangerous blood transfusions into a routine procedure. He informed doctors and nurses how to save our lives. A few years later, Leo Baekeland altered the look and feel of the 20th century. He discovered a brittle, unyielding resin that led to the manufacture of nylons, polyester, and vinyl. He informed billions of us that a new, plastic age had begun. Landsteiner and Baekeland, like all teachers, had special talents.

The second bond between leaders and followers is the specialization of labor. Labor is required to accomplish any worthwhile project. To fulfill a specific goal, we join forces in a social hierarchy. The American Association for the Advancement of Science publishes a magazine, SCIENCE, that bridges the distance between science and citizens. No single person can successfully write, edit, and promote a two hundred page issue every month such as the "Century of the Sciences: 20 Discoveries that Changed our Lives". Therefore, SCIENCE requires a publisher, editors, researchers, artists, salesmen, and distributors. These staff members are divided into functional and geographical departments, each of which has a chain of command. Each person, from the publisher to the mail room clerk, performs specialized duties so that SCIENCE can prosper and pay everyone's salary.

This labor specialization helps empower persons psychologically. Job classifications provide most individuals with a useful personal and social identity. Librarians can feel proud that they earned college degrees and that they help people research information. By contrast, people who live outside the labor market often experience extra emotional stress. Retired, unemployed, and handicapped persons share the same dilemma with the artist in America. They strive for self-esteem, while society at large shuns them. Except for a few strong individuals, this isolation is devastating.

The division of labor gives people choices. In 1928, twenty-seven year old William Paley assumed leadership of United Independent Broadcasters. This company, with twelve employees, supplied ten hours of radio programs each week to sixteen stations. But Paley was a restless, energetic, and easily bored individual. After buying majority interest in the business, he renamed it Columbia Broadcasting System, anticipated the future television revolution, and largely invented mass entertainment. Clearly, Paley chose to lead rather than to follow. He selected to eat, sleep, and dream about communications networks. This benefited his thousands of employees who freely elected to follow him. They would rather enjoy New York Yankees baseball games and Fourth of July picnics than read small print in business reports seven days a week. Fortunately for the followers, Paley was willing to read the tiny print. In return, Paley gained by having refreshed employees on Monday morning. If everyone had to do the same job, be it Paley's or his secretary's, people would be unable to benefit from each other's different energy and commitment levels. As is, persons can often produce a higher quality and a greater quantity of goods and services in concert than alone.

The third bond between leaders and followers is the pursuit of glory. Men and women unite in order to bear children. Likewise, leaders and followers embrace in order to create glory, to give birth to ideals, causes, or purposes greater than themselves.

Many leaders are willing to carve a path to glory. Abraham Lincoln sought to lead America away from the Civil War and towards a unified nation. To achieve this noble goal, he needed an audience for his Gettysburg Address just as much as citizens required him as their director. Charles Babbage, who invented the principles behind digital computers one century before actual machines were built, sought to lead the world away from low technology. To fulfill his high purpose, he required persons capable of translating his ideas into practice. In return, these people needed Babbage. Too often, followers underestimate their role in creating Lincolns, Babbages, and other leaders.

Followers have the power to pick their definition of glory. In recent decades Mohandas Gandhi, the Hindu nationalist leader of India; Fidel Castro, the Marxist ruler of Cuba; Martin Luther King, the Southern Baptist organizer of American blacks; and Adolf Hitler, the Chancellor of Germany possessed a look in their eyes, a tone in their voices, and a charisma in their gestures that many followers interpreted as supernatural, superhuman, or at least extraordinary powers. Each of these persons had a different vision. Each of these leaders orchestrated people's emotions. Each of these highly charged individuals penetrated into the public's subconscious dreams. Each of these men convinced followers that they, the followers, were exceptional players in a heroic drama. And, most importantly, each of these leaders was chosen by many followers. Hitler praised death and intolerance, whereas King preached life and empathy. Both men found a large number of receptive ears.

Glory can be either destructive or creative. Napoleon Bonaparte chose and was chosen to destroy. He rose to the rank of general by inspiring thousands of soldiers to kill and die for him and for his definition of France. Bourienne, Napoleon's trusted and terribly overworked secretary, wrote that his master's troops often could not understand what Napoleon said, but no matter, they would have followed him cheerfully barefoot and without provisions. Napoleon, who was fully aware of people's profound need for a triumphant leader, summarized the loyalty of his followers with these words: "My power depends upon my glory, and my glory on my victories. My power would fall were I not to support it by new glory and new victories." He realized the simple fact that virtually everyone loves a winner.

The greatest victories are creative. In July 1969, people all around the Earth sat mesmerized in front of television sets. Their heartbeats pounded fiercely and their eyes watered with excitement. Before them was one of our species' most glorious moments. Neil Armstrong, a shy and self-effacing hero, stepped onto the powdery surface of the moon and said, "That's one small step for a man, one giant leap for mankind." Armstrong's footprint was made possible by the greatest army ever assembled. That team, the National Aeronautics and Space Administration (NASA), consisted of thousands of soldiers from all walks of life whose high purpose was to travel where no person had ever been. NASA's enemy was the status quo; its ally was progress. Troops of scientists, engineers, and technicians designed, manufactured, and guided the Apollo 11 to the moon by cooperating with each other. Technical experts such as H. Julian Allen, John Houbolt, and Howard Tindall, managers such as Christopher Craft and George Low, and politicians such as President Lyndon Johnson and Congressman George Miller joined hands as they never did before, or after, for the glory of all humanity. Their glory did not require a war worth dying for, but an aspiration worth living for.

Glory is ours to earn. We can team up with inventors, adventurers, and discoverers everywhere who help our species advance. In every field of endeavor, unsung heroes await followers who will sing their praises. Leaders give energy, inspiration, and direction to followers. But only the esteem and devotion of followers endow lasting power and renown to leaders.

The fourth bond between leaders and followers is the ease of conformity. Humans are social animals. This means it is easier for us to live with others than without them. Most people would rather have one more friend than yet another enemy. People join clubs, associations, and groups of every sort in order to share their values. The Affirmist Society, headquartered in California, is an example. It attracts men and women throughout the world who applaud and support uplifting information, labor, and glory within the arts, humanities, and sciences.

Conformity is taught early in life. Children are prompted, coerced if you will, to copy parents, teachers, and peers' behavior and thought. Most American children, for example, conform to society's eating habits. If given the choice, these kids pack their lunchbags with hamburgers rather than with raw fish. Japanese youths chose raw fish. Clearly, social pressure to reproduce other persons' values generates a ready supply of followers. It is less obvious, but equally true, that social standardization produces an ample crop of leaders. This paradox vanishes when we realize that the vast majority of leaders are simply good conformists. These leaders skillfully mirror the masses.

Many prominent leaders excel at conformity. In 1954, a fifty-two year old Chicago milkshake-machine salesman from frugal, middleclass stock visited one of his San Bernardino, California accounts. His name was Ray Kroc. He was curious how his customer sold so many milkshakes. To Kroc's surprise, he found a tiny restaurant that sold hamburgers, french fries, and beverages with a minimum of service. Kroc understood commercial America. The son of a Western Union employee, he immediately intuited that this fast food store was perfectly suited for mobile, impatient Americans who were unimpressed by fancy foods. Kroc approached the owners, Mac and Dick McDonald, and purchased the rights to duplicate their restaurant on a national scale. The rest is history. Kroc built over 7,400 McDonald's food outlets, which made him one of America's half-dozen wealthiest persons. From his 210-acre California ranch and Versailles style Florida home, Kroc looks out at a mass culture which suits his taste. His goal was to provide Americans with the same meal and decor from Atlantic to Pacific, so that they always felt at home. His success is grounded in his unabashed ability to deliver edible conformity.

Leaders conform in one of two primary ways. First, as with Kroc, they genuinely share the traditions and prejudices of their followers. They are "one of the guys." Secondly, leaders mesh with followers in a more

46

calculated fashion. This second form is illustrated in the following election.

In 1932, Iowa's Democratic Party nominated Ola Babcock Miller to run for Secretary of State. Pundits assumed that the sixty-year old widow of a small town newspaper publisher would lose. Afterall, the Republicans had controlled Iowa since the Civil War. But Miller was smart. She asked her son-in-law, a professor and advertising expert named George Gallup, for advice. Gallup's strategy was revolutionary. He sent people door to door to ask voters what they wanted. Next, Miller told the Iowa voters exactly what they desired to hear. She won the election.

The ability to echo public sentiment was refined. Gallup formed the American Institute of Public Opinion. This group began systematically sampling public values. When the institute's poll accurately predicted that Franklin D. Roosevelt would defeat Alf Landon in the 1936 presidental election, the Gallup Poll became an American institution. George Gallup succeeded because he informed leaders what followers wanted. In his own words, "If government is supposed to be based on the will of the people, then somebody ought to go out and find out what the will is."

Gallup's hope that conformity supports democracy is misleading. Unfortunately, there is a darker side to conformity. Life is rough. Many adults are emotionally brutalized by the struggle to earn food and shelter, by their friends' betrayals, and by a hundred common hardships. These men and women become addicted to what Goethe called the most universal emotion, fear. They fear other persons, physical illness, natural disasters, violent crime, their death, and the unknown. Worst of all, they fear deciding their own fate. Many of these followers cry out for heavy-handed authoritarians who demand extreme conformity. They marry persons who boss them around shamelessly and vote for tyrants who censor them ruthlessly. These followers will an undemocratic state.

It is hard to overstate how deeply many followers conform to their leaders. The passion to obey is every bit as intense as the hunger to command. When Soviet dictator Joseph Stalin died, millions of Russians rushed into the streets and cried. Persons whose families had been sent to Siberian labor camps mourned the mass murderer who fomented their nightmares. These rank-and-file citizens deluded themselves that Stalin was innocent of all wrongdoing, that his orders were misinterpreted by zealous subordinates (like themselves). Some persons became hysterical, so habituated were they to the old monster. A second example is equally disturbing.

In 1838, according to author Jean Paulhan, Barbados island staged a strange revolt. About two hundred slaves had recently been emancipated by the Proclamations of March. These freed citizens begged their former master, Glenelg, to return them to bondage. An Anabaptist minister, the spokesman for the group, read aloud a list of grievances. Glenelg, either because he was scrupulous or because he feared government officials, refused to be swayed. Consequently, the former slaves massacred him and his family. The Russian and Barbados followers could face a known, though terrible, leader easier than they could confront an unknown, leaderless life.

Conformity, like good wine, is healthy when consumed in moderation. Excessive social uniformity leads to absurdity, at best, and carnage, at worst. Physicist Alfred Schild captured conformity's ludicrous side when he wrote, "If a wrinkled forehead is ever accepted as a clear sign of a man's devotion to scholarly concentration, our campus lawns will swarm with empty-headed figures vigorously practicing frowns and other facial distortions." Oscar Wilde, the British wit, hinted at conformity's lethal side when he quipped that those who try to lead the people can only do so by following the mob. For better or worse, conformity binds leaders and followers.

I have outlined four bonds between leaders and followers. However, all is not peaceful under the sun. The symbiotic relationship between active persons, who grasp power directly, and passive persons, who crave power indirectly, can provoke distrust and hostility. Let us shine light on the causes of these ill-feelings. There are four basic tensions between leaders and followers: envy, varying degrees of self-confidence, ethical differences, and contrasting views of society.

The first tension between leaders and followers is envy. Many persons cannot stomach to watch their friends, colleagues, or neighbors climb to greater heights than themselves. Envy degenerates into revenge so frequently that a list of examples could fill volumes. But this book is short. Therefore, we shall examine just one case.

Linus Pauling was born in Portland, Oregon in 1901. After graduating from Oregon Agricultural College (now called Oregon State University), he earned his doctorate at the elite California Institute of Technology (Caltech). In the decades that followed, Pauling worked diligently and successfully. He helped discover an artificial substitute for blood serum, helped unravel the cause of sickle-cell anemia, invented an oxygen detector, and contributed pioneer research to several branches of science. In addition, he wrote an influential textbook, THE

49

NATURE OF THE CHEMICAL BOND. In 1954 Pauling, then a Caltech professor and a hero for a generation of scientists, was awarded the Nobel Prize in chemistry.

Pauling used the Swedish award's prestige to affirm life. In particular, he studied radioactive fallout due to the atmospheric testing of atomic bombs. He wrote letters and gave public lectures in many countries explaining the dangerous side-effects of radiation. These humanitarian efforts were greeted by widespread hostility from Americans, who sought glory in an arms race with the Soviet Union. But Pauling marched on. He and his wife circulated a petition worldwide that called for an end to nuclear testing. Over eleven thousand scientists signed his petition. Pauling submitted it to Dag Hammarskjold, secretary-general of the United Nations. For these heroic efforts, Pauling, still a Caltech professor, was awarded the Nobel Peace Prize in 1962.

A healthy, secure Caltech faculty would have given Pauling a hero's welcome. Here was a colleague whose career was dedicated to humanity. Pauling's peace efforts, alone, made life safer for every faculty member's children and grandchildren. Here was a fellow scientist who brought the most favorable worldwide publicity to his colleagues' institution. But envy is irrational and self-destructive. Life is stranger than fiction. Pauling was persuaded to pack his bags and move elsewhere. Twenty-two years later, Pauling directs the Linus Pauling Institute of Science and Medicine near San Francisco. He is an authority on preventive medicine. Little has changed. He is still attacked fiercely by many envious followers whom he works around the clock to help.

The solution to envy is twofold. First, followers should realize that envy is like a cancer that eats away at the spirit. It is a waste of time and energy to dislike persons who have what we think, often mistakenly, that we want. Instead, we should try to emulate those whom we consider more fortunate than ourselves. Conversely, chosen leaders should eagerly assist those followers who have the maturity to help themselves climb upward.

The second tension between leaders and followers is varying degrees of self-confidence. Rulers have, on the whole, much higher self-esteem than their subordinates. Painter Marc Chagall said, ''When I am finishing a picture I hold some God-made object up to it, a rock, a flower... as a kind of final test. If the painting stands up besides a thing man cannot make, the painting is authentic.'' Picasso added, ''There are painters who transform the sun into a yellow spot, but there are others who, thanks to their art and intelligence, transform a yellow spot into the sun.'' Creators Chagall and Picasso shared a rare conviction that, in spite of all obstacles thrown in their way, they and their art would prevail. William Faulkner, author of the immortal THE SOUND AND THE FURY, reiterated this profound belief in the self when he noted that nothing can injure a man's writing if he's a first-rate writer. These three persons reached out across history with the magnetism of natural forces.

It is hard for followers to achieve magnetism. Imagine Chicago clerks who sort mail eight hours a day. The United States government tells them when to work, the American Postal Worker's Union orders them how to labor, and their families inform them how, when, and where to spend their paycheck. The letter and package sorters tend to become passive. Much like art critics under the thumb of an editor, they cannot dictate their own standards. They cannot take big risks, but only tiny ones.

They are perpetually on the defense, reacting to other persons' whims. In short, followers lack clear-cut personal victories that boost their confidence.

The tie between victory and confidence is explicit in Muhammad Ali. Ali was a boxer. After winning the 1960 Olympic Gold Medal at the age of eighteen, he (then known as Cassius Clay) had the nerve to step into the ring with many muscular, fast boxers who wanted to knock him unconscious. He won fifty-six professional fights and the heavyweight championship of the world a record three times. During his prime, Ali was a masterful publicist. One of his ploys was to deliver tongue-in-cheek poems celebrating his well-established greatness as a fighter, such as: "I done wrassled with an alligator/ I done tussled with a whale.../ Only last week I murdered a rock/ Injured a stone, hospitalized a brick/ I'm so mean I make medicine sick." Ali, the son of an uneducated sign painter, predicted the rounds in which he would knock out his foes and starred in a 1977 movie about himself, "The Greatest."

Ali's self-confidence, his natural force, rubbed millions of persons the wrong way. Poor boxers everywhere were angered that a black man from Louisville, Kentucky could not only become famous and wealthy but, worst of all, dared to take credit for his own victories! These persons, trapped in stifling jobs that suffocated their egos, wanted desperately for Ali, "The Big Mouth," to break his jaw and confidence in the ring. When Ali refused induction into the United States Army on the grounds that he was a Black Muslim minister opposed to killing people in Vietnam, he was sentenced to five years in jail and stripped of his heavyweight title. His refusal brought death threats from outraged Americans, persons who routinely excused their own ministers from military duty. Ali also received a letter from philosopher and activist Bertrand Russell, who wrote, "They will try to break you because you are a symbol of a force they are unable to destroy, namely the aroused consciousness of a whole people determined no longer to be butchered and debased with fear and oppression."

The antagonism between more and less self-confident persons can be reduced with empathy. Imagine an enthusiastic, renowned pianist seated beside a demoralized, mediocre cellist at a dinner party. The evening will be better for everyone, if the pianist mixes his pride with humor and if the cellist recalls his most pleasurable moments with cellos. All persons have talents that should merit light-hearted boasts and clumsinesses that should evoke self-humor. Leaders and followers who face both their best and worst qualities are well on the way to a healthy, diplomatic form of confidence.

The third tension between leaders and followers is ethical differences. Ethical systems of all sorts have been preached by theologians and philosophers. But, when sermons are over, people take seriously only those virtues and vices that touch them practically. The maxim "Thou shall not aspire to be a king" sounds terribly abstract, and has zero ethical impact, to New Orleans suburbanites. Insurance salesmen, airline pilots, and technical writers neither meet nor think about kings. However, the same rule very much impressed the 18th century aristocrats who gabbed at Frederick the Great's court. The maxim cautioned these blue bloods to beware of court intrigues and revolutions. It warned them that Frederick, the feared and admired ruler who defeated half of Europe and tore off a limb from Poland just to keep it from Russia, would not take kindly to their competition for his job. Conversely, the ethical rule "Thou shall not gamble" probably carries more weight among Turkey, Texas sheriff's deputies than amidst New York Stock Exchange policy makers.

Tension develops when contrary ethics are brought close together. This happened in 18th century France. Queen Marie Antoinette believed that it was ethical to spend the public treasury on her costly clothes, jewels, palaces, operas, and parties. She thought it totally moral to gamble and loan away fortunes that she did not lift a finger to earn. The Queen, nicknamed Madame Deficit by Parisians, judged it not only proper but noble for aristocrats to ride luxurious carriages throughout France while demanding higher taxes from barefoot peasants. Meanwhile, the peasants and middle class had minds of their own. For them, an ethical society was obliged to provide for the subsistence of all members, either by procuring work for them or by assuring survival to those who were unable to work. On October 16, 1793, executioner Henri Sanson led Marie Antoinette to the guillotine and, at noon, held her severed head before a cheering mob. The French Revolution was underway.

The conflict between ethical systems can be reduced. Traditionally, this is accomplished through secrecy. KGB (Russian secret police) directors and Vatican cardinals do not publicly discuss the attempted assassination of Pope Paul or the sexual sins of Pope Alexander VI, respectively. Both the Soviet and Italian leaders implicitly believe that their followers are incapable of dealing with the genuine facts of life. A more affirmative way to diminish hostility is for leaders to treat followers as valuable persons, rather than as objects to be manipulated. Followers, for their part, should become more cosmopolitan and look beyond the ethical prejudices of their neighborhood.

The fourth tension between leaders and followers is contrasting views of society. For most followers, society is a collection of impersonal businesses, universities, labor unions, and churches that they kneel before. They see the United States Supreme Court as a larger-than-life institution with impartial judges who have mastered the wisdom of the ages. Leaders have a less abstract vision. For them, society's every nook and cranny is personal. Dupont Chemical Company, the University of California, the Brotherhood of Teamsters, and the Baptist Church reflect the successes and failures of their rulers. For leaders, the Supreme Court is nine judges who interpret the Constitution with due respect for their investments, marriages, and dinner guests.

A few leaders view society as their private toy. For John Pierpont Morgan, the Supreme Court was little more than a club of poorly paid social servants. A huge, gruff man with fierce eyes, J.P. Morgan wanted to shape the United States in his image. The financial and political clout that he acquired around the turn of the nineteenth century is impressive. His railroad empire controlled the main transportation network for two thirds of the continent, and his United States Steel Company produced almost 70 percent of the nation's steel. But that was only a start. As a banker, he helped start the General Electric Company and the American Telephone and Telegraph Company. Morgan's America was very personal indeed. The nation consisted of himself and his business associates. What was good for J.P., he thought, was damned good enough for America.

Later, in China, another leader fashioned society around his image. Mao Tze-Tung glorified Chinese peasants and led a revolution to free them from oppressive leaders. After Mao defeated Chaing Kai-shek's regime, Mao set up a new dictatorship in which enslaved "peasants" became liberated "comrades." Mao went further than Morgan. The Chinese leader was able to install himself as a virtual god. Posters of him and quotations from him appeared in public squares and buildings throughout China. For Mao, society was very personal indeed. For his followers, China consisted of a vast army and a communist party apparatus governed by faceless, nameless persons. An elderly Mao confessed to Henry Kissinger, the former American Secretary of State, that all ideology is a means of controlling the masses, of attaining power.

Sooner or later, leaders and followers battle over whom society should personify. Americans, angered at J.P. Morgan and his Robber Barron friends, passed strict anti-trust laws to curb concentrations of wealth. Chinese, tired of Cultural Revolutions and ideological purges, now favor industrialization at the expense of a Mao cult.

We are now at a crossroad. Unquestionably, leaders and followers have both common and dissimilar needs. It is time to affirm how leaders and followers should treat one other, how each of us should act towards those persons who are stronger and weaker than ourselves. The Egyptians believed that one person, the pharaoh, should be the center of all authority, while anarchists advocate total decentralization of power. It is time to find a position between these two extremes.

Affirmists believe that leaders and followers can, and should, coexist in relative harmony. Our goal is not easy. But we have inspiring predecessors. Voltaire, tne French writer and activist, spent decades fighting so that the average person could live with dignity. His enemies, the

56

Versailles aristocracy and the Catholic church, believed that the common man was an uncouth beast to be spurred for the pleasure of a few. Thomas Jefferson, the American farmer and political theorist, struggled to extend public education. His opponents, the industrialists and the Anglican church, profited from cruel child labor and the fusion of Church and State. Alexander Solzhenitzyn, the Russian novelist, writes boldly to foster liberty in his twentieth century motherland. His exilers, the paranoid Kremlin politicians and police agents, prosper with their dictatorship of the proletariat. These three warriors with pens, along with kindred spirits in all walks of life, have done much to expose, and sometimes reduce, the naked exploitation of the masses by an inhumane few.

We advocates of cooperation between the mighty and the masses are a minority. Most nations that cast votes in the United Nations are dictatorships that outlaw voting at home. These regimes have little regard for human rights. They condone brutality in the name of whatever abstract ideology is handy. We affirm that it is to the mutual interest of both leaders and followers to grant all citizens the right to pursue good health, significant work, economic security, friendship, sex love, community recognition, educational opportunity, a developed intelligence, freedom of speech, cultural enjoyment, a sense of beauty, and opportunity for recreation.

When leaders and followers value their reciprocal roles, respect replaces suspicion. The Japanese are dominating the world's automobile and electronics markets in large part because their factory managers and laborers work together as a team. In the United States, industrial supervisors and labor organizers assume an adversary role. This conflict is causing severe economic problems. The same principle exists on a more personal level. Albert Einstein received applications from brilliant scientists who wanted to study under him. He accepted a few. These younger persons offered the founder of relativity fresh ideas and enthusiasm. In return, mentor Einstein gave his proteges experience, inspiration, and reputation. Their relationship was unequal in that Einstein was much more powerful than his followers. But, for persons with a greater purpose in life than flaunting egos, such a disparity is highly positive.

To summarize, wherever there is life there is domination and submission. The firmest oak tree must bend in the wind, or it will crash to the ground and die. The human world is no different. Some people invariably command their environment, whereas others inevitably obey. The vast majority of us live between these extremes. We are, as Shakespeare wrote, actors on a stage who switch roles. Our healthiest, most affirmative attitude is to understand and respect the leaders and followers within each of us. This philosophy leads to a fuller development of the self and a better appreciation of social forces.

IV
APPLAUSE FOR
EARNED IMMORTALITY

"Let mortals rejoice that so great an ornament to the human race has existed!"

—on Newton's tomb

"Immortality is not a gift,
Immortality is an achievement.
And only those who strive mightily
Shall possess it."

—Edgar Lee Masters

People crave immortality. Bedouin camel traders in Saudia Arabian deserts, art conservators in Italian museums, lumberjacks in Finish forests, and book publishers in New York skyscrapers perceive their mission on Earth differently. These colorful members of our noble species prefer food, music, sport, and politics novel to their cultural heritage. So genuine are the differences among them that, when brought together over the centuries, they have succumbed to the nightmare of war more times than humane historians prefer to count. But these diverse people agree on one topic. In one practical sense they are kindred spirits. Namely, they would love to cheat death!

Humans are animals. We are biological organisms composed of bones, muscles, and organs that take approximately two decades to mature. This growing stage is exhilarating but, as does every natural process, it ends. Even for the best athletes, bodies sooner or later deteriorate beyond repair. Compared with boulders in the Swiss Alps that can endure rain, sleet, snow, and sun for millions of years, people are fragile. Humans, as do all other mammals, weather quickly. Contrasted with the giant sequoia trees along California's northern seacoast that can stand strong during thirty centuries of birds singing on their grand branches, people are ephemeral. Our seasons, though more numerous than mayflies, are few.

An Oakland, California resident claims to have been a child when President Abraham Lincoln was assassinated in 1865. If his story is true, he is at least 120 years of age. Scattered between here and China, there are a few other bodies of his vintage. But, for all the billions of persons who have toiled upon the Earth, there is zero scientific evidence that even one human heart has continued beating for two centuries. For most of humanity throughout the ages, and for many impoverished persons alive today, fifty years is a long life span.

Persons fear the shortness of their life span. It is a safe bet that humans do not share this fear with other beasts. My doberman pinscher, named Voltaire, has killed moths and sniffed dead seagulls. But, so far as I can tell, he makes no connection between those deaths and his own. When I asked him if he were immortal, he smiled and searched my pockets for a biscuit. The human Voltaire gave a different answer. He noted, in DICTIONNAIRE PHILOSOPHIQUE, "The human species is the only one which knows it will die, and it knows this through experience." Most children, unless they are reared in war or famine zones, are introduced to death peacefully. One night their grandparent fails to arrive for dinner. A few days later, they attend their first funeral. People learn about death by see-

61

ing and by reading about it. In time, they learn that even the conquerers, kings, and inventors in their history textbooks are no longer walking among us. People conclude, quite reasonably, that death is a universal and inevitable event.

Humans are ingenious creatures. They have devised many ways to allay their fear of imminent death. Generally, persons fall into one of two camps: first, those who believe that they are impotent to confront mortality without gods on their side and, secondly, those who trust that they are powerful enough to face the life-death cycle by themselves. Martin Luther, leader of the German Reformation, was a spokesman for the first camp. He told his followers, in TABLE TALK, "In our sad condition, our only consolation is the expectancy of another life. Here below [below heaven] all is incomprehensible."

Epicurus, a Greek born in the fourth century B.C., had a much more affirmative view of mankind. He taught his students the art of rational living. Epicurus held that most people fear death because it is painful and because their spirit may be forced to experience perpetual torture in a hellish afterlife. He reasoned that both these justifications for fear are unnecessary and avoidable. True enough, a person may be in pain before death. But death itself is as painless as falling into unconsciousness or sleep. The spirit, or "soul" he argued, is merely a particular arrangement of atoms and cannot survive physical destruction. So there can be no eternal pain. This Epicurean attitude points towards the affirmist powerseeker, towards the individual who is willing and able to take responsibility for his actions.

Leonardo da Vinci, the multifacited artist, added to this humane view of life and death in an appealing manner. He asserted that just as a well spent day produces a pleasant sleep, so a well defined life leads to an agreeable death. The objective of life, therefore, should be to foster health and well-being. The best response to life is not to be preoccupied with death, which has as its source human misery, but to affirm the highest qualities of our own lives and of others. His view was lauded and practiced by many figures of the European Age of Reason, especially Condorcet.

Existentialist writers Heidegger and Sartre advised humanity to envision death as a means to heighten our awareness of life. This practical philosophy is evident in Grand Prix race car drivers, test pilots, and mountain climbers, individuals who thrive on danger. These persons are inspired by the razors edge between life and death. Their knowledge of death gives them, as it should the rest of us, a sense of urgency. They should spark us to quit wasting time on trivia and, rather, focus upon what is important to us. Freud appreciated this extra boost. He pointed out that life without awareness of nonlife is as uninteresting as a Platonic romance, or a game played without penalties for defeat and without awards for victory.

Diverse emotional reactions to death have caused humans to invent and embellish a rich marketplace of immortalities over the ages. Educated persons need only read through history and anthropology texts to discover ideologies, religions, and myths that promise their followers heavens of every sort. Before I discuss earned immortality, it is only fair to mention two of our competitors. The first staircase to eternal life remains the most popular one, and the second, for reasons that will be easily grasped, appeals to elite persons who do not wish to overcrowd eternity with commoners.

The first, easiest and most common way to pursue immortality is to ask for it. Millions of followers in every socioeconomic class and geographical region do this daily. They pray to a god that is reputed by leading politicians, priests, and generals to guarantee them a life hereafter in Paradise. In exchange for Holy City, Valhallah, or God's Kingdom, these followers pledge a lifetime of obedience to their leaders in the name of that god. This is one of humanity's oldest methods for binding rulers and subordinates. Sometimes the plea for eternal life is a quiet ceremony. Seekers of immortality kneel before statues, candles, or paintings and whisper sacred words to their god. Followers rarely wonder why their prayer is required, as any omnipotent deity already knows their every feeling and wish, but their words are deemed necessary by leaders. Other rituals are more theatrical.

One of the most colorful pleading rituals involves bleeding. This is said to please Kali, the Indian goddess. Kali is a blood-thirsty woman with hideous fangs, milk filled breasts, cobra necklaces, and an extended tongue. She represents the Terrible World-Mother. With bulging eyes and a short skirt, she dances upon the corpse-like body of the Lord. Eating the entrails of humans or drinking blood from their skulls titillates her tastebuds. Kali, a far cry from the immaculate Blessed Mother that adorns Gothic churches in Italy and vinyl dashboards in the United States, is worshipped in the temple of Kali in Calcutta. Appropriately, her flock slaughters goats in her honor and offers her their blood. Similar sacrifices, often using human virgins, have been practiced in numerous cultures.

Many rulers have always valued kneeling, sacrificing

servants. Therefore, they cultivate ritualized begging for immortality by the powerless masses during war and peace. When cannons are quiet, Machiavellian leaders are able to furnish their palaces with taxes and donations from illiterate peasants and urbanites in return for religious allegories about an afterlife devoid of rich people. In the bloody smoke of war, army commanders assure their terrified soldiers that being crushed by a tank, hacked by knives, or shredded by bullets is a free ticket to the gold-paved, tree-lined boulevards of an eternal paradise. Shiite Moslem suicide squads recently rammed their trucks, filled with explosives, into the Beirut headquarters of the Americans, French, and Israelis. In theory, these Moslems killed themselves in order to find a future bliss more permanent and more pure than life on Earth. They sought death in order to greet their god, Allah, without having to wait in line for death by natural causes.

Suicidal assassins are desperate human beings. To say that such persons merit or receive heavenly reward for their acts is utterly cynical. Muslim, Jewish, and Christian soldiers are ordered to compete in a morbid race to eternal silence.

Powerful persons pay for their own tickets or refuse the ride. They are neither beggars, nor deluded dreamers. They value the conservation of energy. Nothing in life, or in death, is for free. A ruler, or a god, who is unable to provide his devout followers with a fulfilling few decades on Earth is not about to grant eternal bliss for a prayer or a murder. He has neither the desire nor the power to do so. Yet, this logic escapes many persons. The world is full of conformists, who, as Anatole France noted, have no idea what to do with this life, yet want another one that will last forever. If there is a Paradise that accepts lost, confused Earthlings, that Paradise is surely full of complainers who long for greener pastures elsewhere.

Paradise for the asking is too negative for many people. Albert Camus, in THE MYTH OF SISYPHUS, wrote, if there is a sin against life, it consists perhaps not so much in despairing of life as in hoping for another life and in eluding the implacable grandeur of this life. Einstein's NEW YORK TIMES obituary quotes him as saying, "Neither can I believe that the individual survives the death of his body, although feeble souls harbor such thoughts through fear or ridiculous egotisms." In CITY OF LUCCA, Heinrich Heine writes that it must require an inordinate share of vanity and presumption, too, after enjoying so much that is good and beautiful on earth, to ask the Lord for immortality in addition to it all. George Santayana, in THE LIFE OF REASON, observes that the fact of having been born is a bad augury for immortality. Clarence Darrow adds that the origin of the absurd idea of immortal life is easy to discover: it is kept alive by hope and fear, by childish faith, and by cowardice. The list of eminent affirmers of life, not death, goes on and on. For all their differences, these persons share the spirit of Boris Pasternak's immortal declaration: "Man is born to live and not to prepare to live."

A second, more ambitious and rarer way to "escape death" is to proclaim oneself a god. This type of immortality is the prerogative of mental patients and very powerful rulers. The power to call oneself a deity was hinted at in Mesopotamia, often called "the first civilization." In the scorching deserts and barren mountains between the Mediterrean Sea and the Persian Gulf around 3,000 B.C., human culture was considered a gift of the gods rather than an achievement of the people. Leaders told followers that cities were fashioned by gods, who sometimes resided in religious temples within the city's walls. These leaders lived near the god who spoke and acted through them. In reality, these leaders were implicit gods. However, appearances were maintained. Officially, gods were the creators of followers rather than the creations of leaders. Humans were judged, by other humans of course, as subordinate creatures, and even the most powerful persons, the kings, were said to have been appointed by the gods. The idea that a peasant could expect equality in an afterlife that he could not secure on Earth was out of the question. The ordinary follower's best hope, he was assured by leaders, was to attain a gray existence in the underworld.

Man's weakness, that he must grow old and die, was the theme of a popular myth called the EPIC OF GILGAMESH. Gilgamesh, heroically powerful and annoyingly handsome, was said to have been created by the gods and transported from heaven to Earth in order to govern the city of Uruk. Two-thirds god and one-third man, he saw all things even to the ends of the Earth. He underwent all and peered through all secrets. Sometimes this caused concern. Husbands complained that "he leaves not a wife to her master, not a single virgin to her mother." Well, this superhuman playboy was joined by the satyr Enkidu, a man with the strength of a boar, the mane of a lion, and the speed of a bird. Together, they traveled near and far combatting and defeating monsters who personified the forces of nature that threatened humanity. But they were overly enthusiastic and too successful. So the angered council of gods gave Enkidu a mortal illness.

Gilgamesh was upset over the death of Enkidu,

whom he loved more than any woman, and became obsessed with the pursuit of immortality denied his friend. He sought out Siduri, the keeper of a public house, who counciled him to forget his quest and search for something attainable. Eat, drink, and be merry she advised in this passage:

> Gilgamesh, whither rovest thou?
> The life thou pursuest thous shalt not find.
> When the gods created mankind,
> Death for mankind they set aside,
> Life in their own hands retaining.
> Thou, Gilgamesh, let full be thy belly,
> Make thou merry by day and by night.
> Of each day make thou a feast of rejoicing,
> Day and night dance thou and play!
> Let thy garments be sparkling fresh.
> Thy head be washed; bathe thou in water.
> Pay heed to the little one that hold on to thy hand,
> Let thy spouse delight in thy bosom!
> For this is the task of mankind!

Gilgamesh listened, but he wanted more and moved on. Finally, he met Utnapishtim, the Mesopotamian Noah, who recommended that Gilgamesh eat a plant whose fruit would rejuvenate him, if not insure his immortality. Gilgamesh accepted this compromise, having no better option, and proceeded happily home to Uruk. Yet, his homeward journey met disaster. When he stopped to bathe, a snake (worshipped as a symbol of immortality because people believed it could escape death by moulting its skin) stole his plant. Gilgamesh, though a superman, was less than perfect. His one-third human part led him to die.

The Egyptian pharaohs refused to accept Gilgamesh's

mortality or to hide behind gods of their own creation. Bold leaders, pharaohs openly declared themselves gods. They took credit for the creation of villages and cities and, as divine patrons and guardians of their insect-like followers, entitled themselves to the major share of revenues and arable land. With hundreds of thousands of cattle, thousands of slaves, and the religious temple apparatus, the pharaohs resembled the Mesopotamian kings, except in one critical area. The pharaohs did not share power with their priests. Egyptian priests were explicit servants who preached the divinity of the pharaoh in order to receive luxuries. Disobedient priests could be killed or, worse, demoted into a more brutal slavery. The god-pharaohs had sufficient military might to arrest and torture anyone naive enough to call them arrogant, insane, or self-centered.

God-pharaohs were powerful, but not omnipotent. They could not, for example, build pyramids by waving a magic wand or chanting an incantation over the desert sands. Therefore, they did what they could. They waved a whip and barked orders over the backs of thousands of managers, artisans, and rock carriers who designed and constructed grand edifices to house the pharaohs in the life hereafter. These pyramids took many years, and nobody knows how many dead workers, to complete. The largest of the pyramids of Giza, built for Khufu or Cheops more than twenty-five centuries before Christ was a teenager, covered 13 acres and rose over 480 feet from a square base. Truly a magnificent structure. Once completed, the pyramids were as secure from wind, sun, and rain as promised. "All the world fears Time," goes an Arab proverb, "but Time fears the Pyramids." Unfortunately for the pharaohs, their armies were mortal. Their soldiers vanished, and mortal archaeolgists and grave robbers broke into their mortuary chambers. These outsiders discovered all the paraphernalia that the pharaoh might require in his future life. They also found dead humans in pharaoh's caskets.

Ancient Egypt's preoccupation with the afterlife reinforced worldly inequality. A hierarchy of burial places surrounded the pyramid. Nobles, in order to drift through eternity close to their master, were permitted burial in tombs befitting their finances near the pyramid. Peasants, who could not afford tombs, were placed in holes in nearby fields. The slaves who built the pyramids and tombs were not embalmed and mummified carefully enough to share future glories with their pharaoh. They were as expendable in death as they were in life.

The Pharaoh's glorification of dead leaders has a long tradition. Most human gods were, in the beginning, idealized dead men. It was difficult for uneducated, untraveled tribesman thousands of years ago to accept the death of the powerful, wise ruler who led them to victories over men, wolves, and droughts. Once he perished, average followers must have dreamt of him. In these dreams, their chief visited and talked to them. He was, to their superstitious minds, still alive somewhere. That somewhere is in the follower's memory and imagination. That somewhere is the resting place of the Chief, Dracula, and mythical immortals in every culture. Among many primitive peoples, as historian Will Durant noted, the word for god literally meant ''a dead man.'' Even today, among the slightly less superstitious citizens of America and Germany, the commonly used English word SPIRIT and the German word GEIST mean ghost and soul, respectively.

It is a safe bet that you, reader, lack the sociological power to deify yourself and get away with it. This is not to slight you. Many of you have greater economic, technological, and educational power than did humans who ruled as gods in previous centuries. Tycoons among you have more employees than the population of ancient Athens. Politicians amidst you have the weapons to destroy life on Earth. However, your glory faces fierce competition from Christians, Muslims, Marxists, and power seekers everywhere. So you comply with fashion. You call yourself "ordinary folk" and rule the world, un-dramatically, from behind oak doors. Godheads tend to be limited to small cults and fanatical nations. Tastes and fictions change. So, if you are the next god, I hereby apologize for selling you short. I, also, dedicate this book in honor of your radiance. For now, I will address a workable immortality that is within arms reach of we lesser mortals.

The third, most pragmatic way to obtain immortality is to earn it. Earned immortality is accessible to persons at every level of the socioeconomic pyramid. Unlike god-given immortality, it respects intelligence. Unlike god-pharoah immortality, it values labor. Earned immortality is of, by, and for the people. Bertrand Russell wrote that ever since Plato most philosophers have considered it part of their business to produce "proofs" of immortality. They have found fault with the proofs of their predecessors, Saint Thomas rejected Saint Anselm's arguments and Kant rejected Descartes', but they have supplied new ones of their own. In order to make their proofs sound valid, they have falsified logic, made mathematics mystical, and pretended that deep-seated prejudices were heaven sent intuitions. I shall bypass this metaphysical tradition and come directly to the point.

Imagine strolling along a moonlit beach alone. The surf is roaring a few feet away. Stars are twinkling light years distant. The sandy walkway, with its warm and salty breeze, calls out to you. It asks you who you are and how you are improving your corner of this Earth. Maybe your answer is that you are a Chicago schoolteacher during the week and an avid bird watcher on weekends. You help wildlife and fellow humans by lobbying for clean air and national parks. You and your contribution are valuable. Keep walking. Picture your friends, relatives, and fellow workers. Add your children, grandchildren, and unborn generations. Look out to sea. Be honest with yourself. It feels good to trust that someday, while you are alive and after your death, people will walk in your footsteps and remember you. It pleases you that people will remember your classrooms and photographs of birds. To exist in the minds of other humans after our flesh has returned to the land, sea, and sky is an earned immortality worth honoring.

Man is alive! The horrors of war, famine, disease, and ignorance have not stopped us. We have climbed the walls of Buchenwald in order to teach our children kindness, walked past starving Africans on our way to irrigate the Nile Valley, entered hospitals in order to discover a polio vaccine, and soared over bigots on our journey to the moon. We are grandchildren of a noble heritage that has not only endured, but prevailed, for 40,000 generations of hardships and joys. We are worldly enough to be proud. We are too inspired and too great a species to trip over St. Augustine's "Cursed is everyone who places his hope in man" or Nietzsche's "God is Dead!" We are creators and, allied with our cousins the redwood trees and the golden eagles, we are champions. We move onward and upward. For you to remember others' affirmative deeds and they yours helps ennoble our species.

Memory provides people with pleasure as well as an ongoing identity. Everyone writes, with brain cells if not with typewriters, a new entry in his autobiography every day. These notes, some more spellbinding than others, record the dynamic tie between personal habits and ideals. Years ago, an excited young man sat on the library steps at the University of Texas. He had just read a letter offering him his first university teaching position. Today, I remember that person as myself. He walked to the empty Memorial Stadium and, under a bright moon with a bottle of beer, gave a rousing speech to 70,000 heroes and friends, who made him proud to be alive. Afterwards, he shook hands with Goethe and Voltaire. The three of us joked about the hot, humid weather. Later celebrations have reinforced that night in the football stadium. Thinking persons everywhere have their own patterns and rituals. Memory of the past makes the present more meaningful which, in turn, can create a better future.

Memory and habit are related to the brain, a three pound organ surrounded by sensual antennae, much as the Colorado River is allied with the Grand Canyon. The water in the Colorado is continuously changing. Yesterday's water evaporated upward to the clouds, filtered downward towards the bedrock, and flowed southward towards Mexico. Yet, all of this water follows approximately the same route year after year. The water molecules caress the same rocks that they have polished and carved for millions of years. Likewise, experience forms rivulets in the human brain. Some persons have parched channels of bitter memories, while other persons have overflowing streams of joyous recollections. Even for the most imaginative individuals, ideas and actions tend to follow habitual canals that began forming in childhood.

Death destroys habit and memory. Half of this statement provokes little controversy. To be sure, best selling tabloids report about corpses that arise at six o'clock each morning and boil their eggs for precisely four minutes. Ghost, ghoul, and vampire cultists probably take these stories seriously. Fortunately, superstitionists of this variety had their heyday in the Dark Ages. The second half of my assertion is polemic. Millions of persons believe in a socially acceptable "living undead." They argue that dead people have memories, a nonmaterial mind-soul. It is easy to demonstrate that excessive consumption of alchohol can reduce memory, that encephalitis lethargica can make a gentle person cruel, that iodine deficiency can transform a clever child into an idiot, and that lobotomies can diminish severe schizophrenia. If memory cannot survive these relatively mild distortions of the brain, it is a safe bet that it cannot thrive after the total destruction of the brain which occurs at death.

Fortunately, not all minds die at once. Thomas Paine completed his life cycle long before present generations were born. This fact permits power-seekers to learn from the beginning, middle, and final acts of Paine's adventurous life. Paine, one of the first advocates of American independence from England, was born the son of a corset-maker in Thetford, England. Scorned and mocked for decades because he lacked a formal education, he drove himself to become one of the most erudite persons of his era. The middle scene of his life began at age thirty-seven, when he moved to Philadelphia and became the voice of the American Revolution of 1776 with his pamphlet, COMMON SENSE. Later, in England, he published RIGHTS OF MAN, advocating democracy, and was threatened with arrest. So he fled to France, where he promptly became a French citizen, a member of the National Assembly, and a chief spokesman for the French Revolution. All was fine until he voted against the execution of Louis XVI and Marie Antoinette and in favor of their exile. For this, he was declared a colonialist warmonger and tossed into jail. In the final act of his career, Paine returned to America in 1802. The American and French revolutions were already history, and Paine was ignored. Driven to alcohol, he deteriorated terribly and in 1809 died in a New York City lodging house. Paine's failures and victories illustrate an important element of earned immortality, the ebbs and tides of public opinion.

Thomas Paine died long ago, as did his personal memory. However, his life remains in the minds of other persons because of his heroic fight for democracy. He exemplifies the grandest form of earned immortality, that which comes from producing an immortal work, in his case the RIGHTS OF MAN. He is unusual but not unique. Muhammad, orphaned at age six and reared amidst ignorance and poverty, lives forever in the minds of humanity because he authored the Moslem holy scriptures, the KORAN. Euclid, employed as a teacher in Alexandria, Egypt in 300 B.C., and St. Paul, trained as a tentmaker in present-day Turkey, are among us still because they wrote the foundations of geometry in ELEMENTS and the groundwork of Christian theology in the NEW TESTAMENT, respectively. Closer to home, Francis Crick and Thomas Watson will be part of the thirtieth century because of their discovery of the structure of DNA as described in THE DOUBLE HELIX.

These six individuals are obviously rare. Few of us will earn immortality on their scale. Nonetheless, they illustrate three truths that are valuable to all persons who prefer power to impotence. First and foremost, these historical figures were human beings who ate, labored, laughed, and slept as do the rest of us. They did not profess to be gods (though a couple of them were terribly tempted to make that jump). Their lasting contributions are products of extraordinary courage, hard work, and talent. Second, Paine, Muhammad, Euclid, Paul, Crick and Watson gave our species something that it needs. They filled a vacuum, so to speak, with democracy, religion, and science. Third, each had to overcome the inherited prejudices of his era. Each had to persuade others to accept his point of view. All power-seekers start with similar obstacles. They must earn a measure of immortality, a place in other person's minds, by giving (not taking) something valuable to others.

People, from the most bashful bookkeeper to the most flamboyant entertainer, invariably want to be remembered for their actions and thoughts. They desire, whether they admit it or not, to leave a mark on the world. They long to believe that the Earth is a little better planet as a result of their being alive. This healthy impulse, which benefits both themselves and others, is manifested in so many everyday actions that it is easy to overlook. When people bake a chocolate cake for their mother's birthday, they want to enjoy the dessert with her, now, and to give her fond memories of this day. When people take photographs of Eskimos on their vacation in Alaska, they desire to share those experiences with someone in the future.

Bearing and rearing children is the most common way to earn immortality. Biologically, adults pass on their race, facial structure, and hair color to the next century by nurturing offspring who will outlive them. Most adults derive much of their self-esteem from trickling into the human gene pool in this way. Socially, parents aspire to transmit their inherited customs, favorite anecdotes, financial assets, and ethical values through children created in their image. Hundreds of millions of parents work hard to make these biological and social dreams come true. They build homes and plant trees that benefit not only themselves but future persons. These humans strive to extend their life by sacrificing in behalf of, hopefully, appreciative children who have memories.

Cynics say it is ridiculous for persons to concern themselves with the future. They claim it makes no difference whether, or how, persons are remembered by their children or friends. "Live for the moment," they preach. "The future will take care of itself." When persons fall victim to the Great Reaper, they are dead. Period. These misanthropes are wrong. The future is important for two reasons.

First, everyone affects the future. John Muir spent years exploring the Sierra Nevada mountains. The wilderness was his first love. He had a choice. He could have done nothing to preserve the Sierras, or he could have worked to maintain them. Either course of action would have affected the Sierras. Fortunately, John Muir valued the wilderness, humanity, and himself sufficiently to act responsibly towards the future. He fought timber and mining companies, which wanted to cut and blast mountains into an ugly wasteland. As a result, Yosemite National Park exists. Abraham Lincoln also had a choice. He could have become a wealthy slaveowner or an abolitionist. Either decision would have affected slaves. Fortunately, Lincoln selected to act responsibly. Lincoln, like Muir and many parents, was maligned and cursed for openly working to improve the future. Cynics are weak and lazy. They try to hide their head in the sand and avoid responsibility for the impact their benign neglect has on the future. Powerful persons are proud to actively build the future.

Secondly, people are social animals. Much of their self identity is derived by their memory of other persons. This hypothesis is easy to test. Pronounce aloud the names of two friends whom you have not visited for at least one year. Now close your eyes and relive the most powerful single experience that each name evokes. The mental pictures that you have recalled help make your friends, and you, human. If you remembered no one, you would have a biological past, as does a tree, but not a human history. At best, you would be a terribly lonely person.

Memory empowers us to survive. The ability to retain and reproduce mental and sensory data at will is a necessity, not a luxury. A sociologist who awakens one morning in London to find her identification papers stolen is merely inconvenienced. But, if she has no memory of her name, her residence, or her employer, she is in serious trouble. Amnesia debilitates her as quickly and thoroughly as a paralysing automobile accident. Without memory, her complex social world degenerates into utter chaos. She finds herself surrounded by bellhops and tourists who look like her but with whom she cannot relate. If not cared for by other persons, the vacationer without a name will be destroyed by natural causes or predators in short order. Even a hermit living in a Rocky

Mountain cave needs the past in order to insure a future. He will die in a few days, if he forgets the difference between acorns, blackberries, and poisonous mushrooms.

Memory enables us to grow. Astronomer Carl Sagan estimates that the human brain stores perhaps one hundred trillion pieces of data. Imagine typing a letter of the alphabet, a punctuation mark, or an empty space 100,000,000,000,000 times. This massive typing project would fill twenty million books, the number of volumes found in the world's largest libraries. This Library of Congress sized collection exists between each person's ears. Of course, some persons have fewer blank pages and damaged volumes than others. But even a weak brain, in concert with eyes, ears, nostrils, tastebuds, and nerve endings, houses an amazing array of instincts and acquired skills.

In addition, society has a collective memory. Libaries and teachers transmit this cultural history so that humans do not have to reinvent stone fireplaces, wax candles, and incandescent lightbulbs every generation. Collective memory enables curious persons to learn from the errors and successes of their ancestors. The most courageous, talented and hardworking of these individuals go on to invent ultraviolet lamps, lasers, and other revolutionary sources of light. They enable society to grow. More commonly, memory insures that persons do not have to waste energy rediscovering how to tie their shoes and brush their teeth every morning. They can move forward.

Memory inspirits people to dream. When inquisitive persons flip through photographs of horse drawn carriages, their minds are kindled. They wonder how two hundred horse power autos will appear to future generations and fantasize about what will replace these gasoline fueled vehicles. When they study old world maps, they are jolted that humans thought a mountain range in Mongolia or in Peru was the edge of the universe. They ponder what worlds are still unknown. For a hundred thousand years, most humans were positive that there was little in the Cosmos except the Earth. Now, in the last fraction of one percent of the existence of our species, many persons know better. The future remains, as it always has been, mysterious because the options and horizons are unlimited. As T.H. Huxley noted in 1887, ''The known is finite, the unknown infinite; intellectually we stand on an islet in the midst of an illimitable ocean of inexplicabilty. Our business in every generation is to reclaim a little more land.''

People are detectives who want clues about where their islet fits into the grand jigsaw puzzle. Their search is rough. For one thing, individual and social memories are relatively short. When persons eat oranges, their brain programs and supervises every biochemical step necessary to transform that citrus fruit into body tissues. Peoples' genetic memory, which works silently and invisibly, has evolved over millions of years. By comparison, individual memory begins shortly after birth and lives only a few decades. Social memory fares a little better. The most educated persons can analyse and synthesize but a few thousand years of human history.

Immortality is earned by persons who esteem individual and social memory. These persons embody past realities and future potentialities. Isaac Newton, arguably the most influential scientist who ever lived, was one person who valued memory. Born in 1643, the year after Galileo died, Newton was reared in the soil and toil of the seventeen century. His era was reflected by Bacon's AD-

80

VANCEMENT OF LEARNING and Cervantes' DON QUIXOTE, both published in 1605, and by the first edition of HAMLET, which appeared in 1606. But Newton was not merely a product of his times. He took the energy to look backward, to stand upon the shoulders of giants who had preceded him. Newton studied his immortal predecessors, while others were "too busy" to waste their time with dead generations. He learned from Copernicus, Pythagoras, and Lagrange. When stumped by an illustration in a book, Newton did not toss the problem aside and look for an easier puzzle. Rather, he explored centuries backward into social memory. He found a copy of Euclid's ELEMENTS OF GEOMETRY and read it until the illustration made sense. Two years later, Newton invented differential calculus. When Newton read of Johannes Kepler's futile attempt to predict the motion of the planets, he did not throw his arms into the air in despair. Rather, he studied other immortal persons' celestial models. This going back in time helped him deduce the nature of gravitational force.

Newton provides an invaluable lesson. Namely, he illustrates that whoever wishes to go forward in history must know, first of all, where he has come from. The architect, composer, or football coach who understands the history of building materials, musical instruments, and gridiron strategy has much more power to innovate than ahistorical colleagues. The future does not exist in a vacuum, any more than the present does. Humanity landed astronauts on the moon only because of a long series of events, beginning with observant persons who realized that the moon revolves around the Earth. To be remembered by others, persons must contribute to the ties between past and future. This takes work and integrity.

People cannot expect to earn immortality, if they are too lazy and too self-centered to remember what others have done for them.

Earned immortality affirms human nobility. It reminds us that we are part of a great chain of events. As I wrote in the AFFIRMIST MANIFESTO, "Man's purpose is to affirm truth and, by standing on the shoulders of courage and genius, to climb heroically in a Cosmos indifferent to our existence." Good architects, composers, and football coaches are similar to Newton in that all of them strain themselves to climb ontop the shoulders of adventurous and innovative predecessors.

Applause for earned immortality is dissuaded by many societies. American magazines, newspapers, and television programs are obsessed with popularity and notoriety contests. In search of advertising dollars that require new faces and themes, the media bombard the public with a collage of "personalities." One month Daniel Ellsberg, who released the scandalous PENTAGON PAPERS revealing America's secret role in the Vietnam War, is omnipresent. His photos, interviews, and friends are everywhere people look and listen. The next month Erica Jong, author of the sexual novel, FEAR OF FLYING, is the talk of the nation. She, in turn, gives ways to Vicki Morgan, the mistress of a famous businessman, or whoever is convenient. This revolving door of celebrities prompted Andy Warhol, a New York artist and masterful media manipulator, to pronounce that someday everyone will be famous for fifteen minutes. The dizzying speed with which people come and go farcifies earned immortality.

America's preoccupation with hype and trivia is only one way to assault earned immortality. The Soviet Union uses a heavier hand. Communist party bureaucrats simply rewrite history according to their whims. One day Andrei Sakharov is a national hero for helping develop nuclear weapons. Another day he is under house arrest in Gorky as an enemy of the state for advocating international peace. One moment Nikita Krushchev is the nation's leader. The next moment his name is scratched from history books.

Powerful propagandists strive to erase individual and social memory of immortal persons. Sometimes these leaders use subtle psychological methods, sometimes brutal military tactics. Whatever the ploy, many leaders deny their followers a healthy balance between the past, present, and future. The motivation of Machiavellian rulers is as easy for us to affirm as it is for them to negate. Immortal persons are threatening. Homer's THE ODYESSEY and Arthur Clarke's 2001: A SPACE ODYSSEY intimidate dogmatists. Insecure leaders fear, rightfully so, that lasting works expose and undermine their mediocre authority. Thus, they carry on a war against the heroic tradition of humanity. They attempt to bully citizens into joining their campaign. Virtually everywhere, average citizens are libeled and slandered. These followers, many of whom are valuable persons, are told that they are too stupid to appreciate the contributions of their best predecessors and too insignificant to add to the future.

Widespread censorship has disastrous side-effects. People who are deterred from valuing their cultural forefathers and the founders of new ideas are lost. They are unconscious of their place on this Earth. They are thrown into a vicious cycle of confusion and low self-esteem. They are made impotent to act effectively. They are denied the opportunity to leave a mark in this life. In return, they are told to beg their leaders for a future Paradise.

Future readers of this book will be diverse. A few, who are not yet born, will command space fleets that gather asteroids for masonry, dismantle planets for precious metals, or employ white dwarfs for gravitational propulsion. They will look back at landing men on the moon as child's play. Other readers will wash dishes on space stations and question why they are not admirals in intergalactic space. Children will take pills that immunize them against cancer and other dreaded diseases. They will judge us primitive for tolerating such ailments. Wherever they might be, reflective readers will seek to make sense of their birth, death, past, present, and future. A few of them will appreciate us, just as a minority of us value those who have come before us.

To reiterate, fear of death is a widespread phenomenon that provokes numerous approaches to immortality. To beg, to declare, and to earn immortality are three responses to death. Only earned immortality respects the intelligence and labor of a broad spectrum of leaders and followers. It is an honor and a duty to improve our corner of the world and to celebrate others who do likewise. To appreciate persons who leave gardens, buildings, memories, and works of art for the rest of us to enjoy is part of being fully human. We applaud earned immortality.

V
THE VIOLENT CRY
OF IMPOTENCE

"The more the drive towards life is thwarted, the stronger is the drive towards destruction; the more life is realized, the less is the strength of destructiveness. Destructiveness is the outcome of outlived life."

—Eric Fromm

"Violence is here,
In the world of the sane,
And violence is a symptom,
I hear it in the headlong weeping of men who have failed.
I see it in the terrible dreams of boys
Whose adolescence repeats all history."

—Jacob Bronowski

Humans are helpless at birth. They are wanting in sexual power, the ability to reproduce their kind, and they are impotent in countless other ways. They cannot clean their diapers, harvest their cereal, or build their cribs. Newborn babies are bundles of potentialities, small creatures with bright eyes and bald heads who make adults giggle and act as children. The good news is that many of these babies will acquire sufficient power to become life-affirming adults. The bad news is that many other children will remain powerless for their entire lives. This second group will grow into neurotics, criminals, terrorists, or other life-negating adults. They will scream out against life. This essay will explore the violent cry of impotent persons.

As to our weaknesses, priests tell us that we are born into original sin; therapists tell us that our parents are to blame. Both are wrong. Power, the ability to produce an intended effect, is an acquired skill. It is natural and healthy that human babies require about twenty years to learn power. Newly hatched alligators can swim and hunt a few minutes after birth, and tadpoles reach maturity in a matter of months. However, for countless generations, adult alligators and frogs have done little more than bask in the sun and eat. To the best of my knowledge, these creatures have little language or culture. They have yet to invent the wheel, much less to launch a space probe past Jupiter. I am not slighting reptiles or amphibians. All animals play a vital role in the balance of nature. Other animals simply illustrate a vital truth; to wit, humans are weak at birth only by comparison with what they can accomplish as adults. Even Isaac Newton was born with his eyes shut.

With foresight, labor, and a bit of luck, you can attain at least a majority of the twelve ingredients of a good life: physical health, significant work, economic security, friendship, sex love, community recognition, educational opportunity, a developed intelligence, freedom of speech, cultural enjoyment, a sense of beauty, and opportunity for recreation. These values assume, of course, that you have more than a modicum of "joie de vivre." Balanced, fulfilling lives go only to persons who are capable of controlling their fates to a large degree.

Some persons are not and do not want to be in charge of their lives. They refuse to accept responsiblity. One such person was the infamous criminal, Charles Manson. By the age of thirty-two, Manson had spent seventeen years in prison. This led him to declare repeatedly, "Prison is my home, the only home I have." In 1967, Manson realized that he was incapable of contributing to society. He begged California authorities not to release him from prison.

Prison officials set Manson upon us anyway. And it was not long until the time bomb inside him exploded. On August 9, 1969, Manson and member sof his "family" cult cut the telephone wires and broke into a secluded home in one of Los Angeles' most fashionable neighborhoods. Once inside, they shot, stabbled, and bludgeoned five persons to death. When Hollywood actress Sharon Tate, eight months pregnant, pleaded for the life of her child, one of the killers replied, "Look, bitch, I have no mercy for you." This merciless family, which worshipped Manson and called him Jesus Christ, killed again and again before they were finally captured. Manson boasted that he had murdered thirty-five persons.

Manson exemplifies failure turned into rage. In this regard, he had much in common with one of his heroes, Hitler. Both suffered because of illegitimacy (Manson was a bastard, as was Hitler's father); both were racists (Manson hated blacks. If his prison record is accurate, he may have thought his father was black. Hitler hated Jews because, according to historians, he was obsessed that he had a Jewish ancestor); and both were frustrated artists (Manson wanted to be a musician, Hitler a painter). Both were vegetarians; both were fascinated by the occult; and both had others kill for them. Both Manson and Hitler surrounded themselves with desperate servants, and both controlled their devotees with hypnotic eyes and repetitive slogans. Both failures even had a favorite curse for their enemies: "pigs" for Manson and "Schweinhund" for Hitler. These similarities provoked Manson to tell his followers that Hitler had the best answers to life.

The American public fixated on Manson for months. His photograph and articles about him were on every newsstand. Before he went on trial, the underground press debated whether Manson was a monster or a revolutionary martyr. ROLLING STONE, a national magazine, issued "A Special Report: Charles Manson, The Incredible Story of the Most Dangerous Man Alive," while TUESDAY'S CHILD, a Hollywood newspaper, proclaimed: "Man of the Year: Charles Manson." Both publications placed the mass killer's face on their covers. While Manson was on trial, millions of citizens followed every detail with an uncanny personal interest. For many of these persons, the modern industrial world is too crowded and complex to cope with. They feel valueless and isolated. They cannot find an authentic purpose for their lives. Life, for them, is a false facade that threatens them much as life scared Manson. The Manson phenomenon reminds us that almost one American in twelve will spend a portion of life in a mental institution.

Fear is a major cause of this dismal mental health statistic. Fear is the rule, not the exception. Most persons live with specific fears of punishment, starvation, unemployment, and illness. These relatively rational fears are nothing more than feelings of lack of power to avoid punishment, starvation, unemployment, and illness. Fear can, also, be irrational. Franklin Delano Roosevelt realized this when he stated that people have nothing to fear but fear itself. Imagine a terrified person hanging from a frayed rope over the Grand Canyon. Now visualize the same person terrorized, not while suspended in space, but while lying on a couch in front of the television set or while walking down the street. Such persons are very common.

A graphic example of generalized helplessness is provided by Henry James, Sr., the father of the philosopher and psychologist William James. The following account

appears in THE LITERARY REMAINS OF THE LATE
HENRY JAMES, which was edited and introduced by his
son:

One day... towards the close of May, having eaten a
comfortable dinner, I remained sitting at the table after
the family had dispersed, idly gazing at the embers in
the grate, thinking of nothing, and feeling only the ex-
hilaration incident to a good digestion, when suddenly,
in a lightening-flash as it were, ''fear came upon me,
and trembling, which made all my bones to shake.'' To
all appearance it was a perfectly insane and abject terror, without ostensible cause, and only to be accounted
for, to my perplexed imagination, by some damned
shape squatting invisible to me within the precincts of
the room and raying out from his fetid personality in-
fluences fatal to life. The thing had not lasted ten
seconds before I felt myself a wreck; that is, reduced
from a state of firm, vigorous, joyful manhood to one
of almost helpless infancy. The only self-control I was
capable of exerting was to keep my seat. I felt the
greatest desire to run incontinently to the foot of the
stairs and shout for help to my wife, to run to the road-
side even, and appeal to the public to protect me; but
by an immense effort I controlled these frenzied impulses, and determined not to budge from my chair till
I had recovered my lost self-possession. This purpose
I held to for a good long hour, as I reckoned time, beat
upon meanwhile by an evergrowing tempest of doubt,
anxiety, and despair, with absolutely no relief from any
truth I had ever encountered save a most pale and distant glimmer of the divine existence, when I resolved
to abandon the vain struggle, and communicate without more ado what seemed my sudden burden of in-
most, implacable unrest to my wife.

90

> Now, to make a long story short, this ghastly condition
> of mind continued with me, with gradually lengthening
> intervals of relief, for two years, and even longer.

The perfectly insane and abject terror that gripped James frightens many persons for their entire lives. For much of humanity, which is unable to overcome the dark side of its character, life is lorded over by ghosts, by personifications of impotence.

Life is full of challenges. Sometimes we win. At other times we lose. Strong persons learn as much from their failures as their successess. Failure, as the English poet Keats noted, is the highway to success inasmuch as every discovery of what is false leads us to seek earnestly after what is true, and every fresh experience points out some form of error which we shall afterward carefully avoid. Weak persons cannot confront failure in this healthy manner.

A person is partially defeated whenever he does not attain a specific goal. This failure is usually mild and soon forgotten. The employee who does not get promoted, the athlete who loses a game, and the investor who picks the wrong stock are common examples. Moderate setbacks are part of everybody's daily life. Trouble begins when minor defeats increase in number, while triumphs decrease. A negative psychology begins to root. A person habitually unable to fulfill chosen ambitions loses dignity. Happiness, the feeling that one's power is increasing, seems more and more remote. A feeling of worthlessness begins to pervade his character. Inner tension builds within him much the way water rises behind a dam. Active resentment, or worse, emerges.

Many such persons are powerless to climb out of the vicious cycle of defeat. They can no longer perform that act which they most desire: to create beyond themselves. They are denied the real reaction to life, that of the positive deed, and they compensate with an imaginary revenge. In order to prove themselves viable, they lash out against the world. Violence is their only way to leave a mark.

On January 26, 1948, Sadamichi Hirasawa walked through the snow in American-occupied Tokyo. The Teikoku Bank was just about to close for the day when he, wearing a white doctor's coat, politely handed his calling card to the chief clerk. The card gave his name as Dr. Jiro Yamaguchi. The imposter explained to the bank's manager that he was attached to General Douglas MacArthur's Occupation Headquarters and that he had orders to immunize the bank's employees against amoebic dysentery. When the employees were gathered into the manager's office, Hirasawa squirted liquid into everyone's drinking mug. "Now," he said. "This medicine is very potent and may burn your throats a little. Gulp it down when I give the word, and I will then give you a dosage from the second bottle. You will then be immune from dysentery."

The fifteen obedient staff members drank first and second doses. Within seconds, they began to choke and fall to the floor. As promised, they were becoming immune to dysentery. The fatal cups of potassium cyanide had begun to act. Meanwhile, Hirasawa emptied the cash registers.

At his trial, the court learned that Hirasawa was once a very talented artist who had been lionized. But, because of a brain disease called Korsakov's syndrome that he contracted after being injected with an anti-rabies serum, Hirasawa's skill had been sapped. The better salons and

92

galleries had begun to reject his work, and his chief patron had died. Hirasawa was surrounded by failure. His two mistresses kept demanding money, and he was going broke. Desperate, Hirasawa thought murder and robbery were the only ways he could maintain his social position. For his irrational efforts, he was sentenced to hang.

Some impotent persons are irrational on a larger scale. In the 1950's, one American lacked the power to face his mortality in a healthy manner. He had a pathological fear of growing old and dying without friends. His name was Joseph McCarthy. In order to feel less lonely, this United States Senator fabricated a "communist conspiracy" (an imagined object for his revenge) and claimed to possess lists of prominent Americans who were aiding the causes of the Soviet Union and other enemies of this nation. McCarthy, with enormous publicity and without a shred of evidence, labored day and night to blacklist and destroy authors, businessmen, scientists, intellectuals, film producers, reporters, and whomever he disliked in the name of patriotism. With his charismatic support, various committees of Congress ran wild throughout the nation. The House Un-American Activities Committee, the Senate Subcommittee on Internal Security, and the Senate Permanent Subcommittee on Investigations constantly undermined the Bill of Rights in order to hunt down and frighten scapegoats, nonconformists, of every sort. In the ironic spirit of communist dictatorships, McCarthy's followers pushed for loyalty oaths and passport denials.

McCarthy's subversion of freedom of assembly, press, and speech extended to every region of the nation. Classrooms, newspapers, news programs, courtrooms, movies, magazines, theatres, art galleries, and publishers were all directly affected. His repression in the name of democracy caused Albert Einstein, held suspect for being more intelligent than leading Congressmen, to advise all thinking persons to follow the nonviolent approach of Gandhi and to risk jail and economic ruin in the interest of American culture, rather than to testify before a group of dangerously insecure, self-destructive members of Congress. Simultaneously, millions of frightened citizens who saw demons under every rock and every bed sheet cheered McCarthy as their hero. McCarthy was their savior, the demagogue who allowed them to carry on business as usual without having to bother with the truth about themselves and the world.

Fortunately, bad times come to an end, and negative persons fade away. Joseph McCarthy had a nervous breakdown and babbled incoherently in front of a crowded Capitol Hill room. Psychologically naked, McCarthy demonstrated his longstanding impotence in the most explicit of terms. He was not fighting communism, but his own sense of failure. He did not resent Russians or Chinese, but people everywhere who did not befriend him. He was alone, in the end, just as he had always feared.

Some impotent persons are absolutely irrational. Enter Hitler. For years, the would-be architect and painter lauded Germany as the pinnacle of civilization and massacred millions of persons in the name of his beloved Third Reich. When the Allied victory was near, Hitler confessed to Albert Speer, "If the German nation is now defeated in this struggle (World War II), it has been too weak. That will mean it has not withstood the test of history and was destined for nothing but doom." This statement had a precise meaning. Hitler, knowing he was powerless to give the world anything positive, wanted to destroy everything and everyone possible. He desired total catastrophe, what Speer called a Wagnerian Gotterdammerung that would prove a genocidal funeral pyre to mark his departure from the stage of history. To accomplish this last goal before his death, Hitler commanded Speer's ministry to annihilate German industry, transportation, communication, and agriculture. Hitler wanted all his followers to starve to death for denying him victory. Hitler, a maniac with millions of screaming supporters, cried out for the absolute impotence of universal death.

Many persons, perhaps Hirasawa, McCarthy, and Hitler, are born into hardship. Maybe their legs were crippled, their skin was the wrong color, their neighborhood was poor, their nation was at war, or their parents were against education. Maybe their father was a despotic alcoholic who demanded that they dominate everyone and, in the same breath, submit to his caprices. There are a thousand and one obstacles. People are born into trouble and contend with it all their life. There is a cry at the beginning of life and a groan at the end of it. As Socrates noted, if all the misfortunes of mankind were cast into a public stock, in order to be equally distributed among the whole species, those who now think themselves the most unhappy would prefer the share they already have to that which would fall to them by such a division.

Weak persons are defeated by misfortune; but powerful persons rise above it. Many children are traumatised for life by early disadvantages. Many others are spoiled for life by childhood luxuries. These normal children become bitter and envious. The natural helplessness of childhood is reinforced, step by step, until powerlessness becomes a lifelong habit. A few children, face-to-face with peril, are jolted wonderously to esteem life. These gifted children, born into the affirmative power-urge, begin restructuring their emotional, personal universe years before they can secure the resources to remold the sociological world. These power-seekers agree with the poet Rilke that what is required of them is that they love the difficult and learn to deal with it.

Temujin was one disadvantaged child. When he was nine, his father was poisoned to death. Temujin's broken-down family endured years of deprivation and starvation. The boy hunted mice for supper. Illiterate, Temujin was kept alive by his mother's stories about the heroic past. These tales obsessed him with the desire to bend the will of others. Toward this end, he organized feuding Mongolian chieftains into a formidable military machine that conquered a vast territory from the Caspian Sea on the west to the Pacific Ocean on the east. Temujin, the world's most feared man, gave posterity this message:

> A man's highest job in life is to break his enemies, to drive them before him, to take from them all the things that have been theirs, to hear the weepings of those who cherished them, to take their horses between his knees, and to press in his arms the desirable of their women.

Temujin (called Genghis Khan, "the universal emperor," by his followers) was a dictator who decided who would live and who would die. It sounds contradictory, at first, to call such a person impotent. Nonetheless, Khan demonstrates the fact that absolute impotence corrupts absolutely. If a man goes into a grocery store and shoots ten people at random, most people will agree that the killer is a maniac. However, if a psychopath marches

96

across an international border and massacres ten thousand persons, the same intelligent persons will judge him a powerful person. Affirmists reject this illogic. To kill one person or one million persons is not a powerful act. It is very easy to murder, and everybody dies anyway. To help people die is no accomplishment. Khan was a thwarted person because he took more from this world than he added. He rose to leadership because weakness was as commonplace in twelfth century Mongolia as it is today. Nobody channeled Temujin's high energy hatred into affirmative action.

Eric Hoffer also had a hard life. Blind in childhood, he was told at the age of nine that his parents' genes insured that he would not live past the age of forty. "When I was almost twenty," Hoffer recalls, "My life was half over, so what was the point of getting excited about anything? I didn't have the idea that I had to get anywhere, that I had to make anything of myself.... So I bought a bus ticket to Los Angeles, and I landed on Skid Row, and I stayed there for the next ten years."

Somehow Hoffer climbed out of the cycle of failure. He recovered his eyesight and became a voracious reader. Hoffer, a common laborer without formal education, read broader and deeper than many of America's and Europe's leading intellectuals. In 1951, the social philosopher published THE TRUE BELIEVER and gained both an enthusiastic readership and critical acclaim. After being interviewed on television in 1967 by Eric Sevareid, Hoffer became a cultural hero. He went on to publish six more books.

Francois Marie Arouet, also, reacted affirmatively to childhood disabilities. A youngest child, Francois was so sickly his first year that nobody thought he would live.

Throughout childhood he was unable to compete physically with other children. However, he transformed adversity into prosperity. He read and wrote during his bed-ridden days and nights. In time, Francois (better known by his adopted name, Voltaire) used his enormous talents to become the Conscience of Europe and one of history's greatest champions of liberty and dignity. Rather than murder persons to release his tension, he helped humanity. Voltaire's tolerant attitude is captured with these words:

> May the trifling differences in the garments that cover our frail bodies, in the mode of expressing our ... thoughts, in our ridiculous customs and imperfect laws... in a word, may the slight variations that are found amongst the atoms called men not be used by us as signals of mutual hatred and persecution!...May all men remember that they are brothers!

Voltaire was a builder, not a destroyer. He gave more to others than he took from them. Voltaire was a victor teaching victory; Khan a victim victimizing.

The belief that life is ultimately senseless is echoed in many immortal literary works. Shakespeare's Macbeth cries out upon hearing the death of his wife:

> Life's but a walking shadow, a poor player
> That struts and frets his hour upon the stage
> And then is heard no more: it is a tale
> Told by an idiot, full of sound and fury,
> Signifying nothing.

Macbeth's cry is echoed in William Faulkner's THE SOUND AND THE FURY. In this novel, the Mississippi author portrays with vivid realism the lives of some of the most famous fictional characters in American literature, the Compson family: Benjy, the idiot man-child; Quentin, the young man who cannot face his heritage; Jason, the cold, brutal realist; Caddy, the rebellious girl loved by her brothers; and Dilsey, their black servant. Faulkner takes his readers through the dissolution of this family. Throughout the novel, he sees humans as weak creatures incapable of rising above their selfish needs. Modern man is pictured as inadequate to cope with the problems of life. This novel is a long way from Faulkner's affirmative, later view that man will not merely endure: he will prevail.

The chronic complainer who curses the unjust universe, the mass media addict who extols the latest fad, the bigot who hunts the next scapegoat, the braggart who magnifies the smallest act, the cynic who mocks the heroic triumph, and the idle dreamer who loathes practical details love to wallow in professional hopelessness, intellectual ennui, and political cynicism. At worst, their sound and fury result in assaults, feuds, suicides, homicides, or large scale genocides. At best, they bore and wear down acquaintances who have the misfortune to cross their paths.

Cunning defeatists are hard to see. They are human chameleons who blend into their environments very well. Masters of camouflage, they not only conceal their inner bankruptcy but promote themselves as the very opposite of whom they are. For years, Theodore Robert Bundy impressed persons that he was an ideal son, an excellent student, a sensitive social worker, and a bright light in the Republican Party. Women considered him as handsome and romantic as a movie idol, and men judged him a young man with a golden future. Well, it turns out that Bundy was a psychopathic killer who left women's dead bodies scattered across the United States. Everyone, including a former policewoman and crime writer who confided to him, was shocked. Bundy summarized himself with these words:

> Society wants to believe it can identify evil people, or bad or harmful persons, but it's not practical. There are no stereotypes. The thing is that some people are just psychologically less ready for failure than others.

Jim Jones was an even more notorious example. Jones was reared in Lynn, Indiana. His father was a railroad man, whom some say was a member of the Ku Klux Klan. His mother was reportedly an anthropologist who gave up her career after dreaming that her son would change the world. Jim's favorite childhood game was "preacher" which he played before neighborhood children. His sermons were moving, and he often called for corporal punishment against those congregation members who displeased him.

As an adult, Jones became a Methodist preacher in Indiana and fought for the civil rights of black people. This cause made him very unpopular and subjected his church to frequent attacks. By the late 1950s, Jones began to vent anger and paranoia. He demanded that parishioners call him "Father" or "Dad" and formed an interrogation committee to drive away anyone who criticized him. His associate minister recalls that Jones threw the Bible on the floor during one sermon and complained, "Too many people are looking at this instead of me."

By the 1970s, Jones was well-established in the San Francisco Bay Area. His congregation, called People's Temple, had two radically different faces. Rebellious members claimed that Jones routinely drugged women and forced them to satisfy his bizarre sexual fantasies. He also laughed while adults beat children four and five years old while the kids screamed into a microphone. Jones devised humiliations and medications that made people appear to die (later to be resurrected by Jones).

Outraged temple members pleaded from 1976-1978 with the press, public officials, and the federal government to expose Jones as a threat to the community. Nobody listened. Most persons were impressed by Jones the confidence man, the public performer. California politicians and public figures stood in line to praise "the tremendous character and integrity" of Reverend Jones. It was not until Jones ordered the assassination of United States Congressman Leo Ryan and commanded 900 People's Temple members to drink lethal poison in Jonestown, South America that people were willing to listen to reality.

Jones, Bundy, Manson and countless others like them are able to thrive because decent people lack the power to see them for what they are and to channel their violence into affirmative endeavors.

Violence seduces many persons who have no haven, solace, or inner peace. The purpose of such violence is to disorient or destroy others; that is, to take away the safe places, comforts, and serenity of others. Because they themselves suffer, perpetrators want to inflict pain as a form of justice. This is illustrated by the schoolyard bully who, because he is beaten regularly by his father, kicks a well-behaved classmate in order to teach the latter how pain feels. Other initiators of pain vandalize storekeepers who catch them stealing and lie to voters who put them in office.

It is a mistake to view violence only as a physical force. Violence, the destructive eruption of pent-up passion, can be subtle as well as brutal. As Nietzsche noted, persons who have not witnessed hands that kill gently have not experienced life.

Mental cruelty is more common than physical abuse. For one thing, it is safer to damage a person's feelings than limbs. The former is difficult to prove in a courtroom, and many jurors have little sympathy for persons injured by words. "Sticks and stones can break my bones, but words can never hurt me," goes the childhood saying. Nonetheless, the pain associated with psychological abuse can be just as intense and crippling as bodily bruises or broken bones. Many people derive pleasure from humiliating others. Mental sadism is practiced by countless parents upon their children, teachers upon their students, and supervisors upon their underlings throughout the world.

Joseph Stalin, the Russian dictator who never overcame the childhood beatings given him by his father, is an outstanding historical example of a thorough sadist. Here are a few examples supplied by R.A. Medvedev, in LET HISTORY JUDGE:

> Shortly before the arrest of the Civil War hero D.F. Serdich, Stalin toasted him at a reception, suggesting that they drink to "Bruderschaft" (brotherhood). Just a few days before Bliukher's destruction, Stalin spoke of him warmly at a meeting. When an Armenian delegation came to him, Stalin asked about the poet Charents and said he should not be touched, but a few months later Charents was arrested and killed. The wife of Ordzhonikidze's Deputy Commissar, A. Serebrovskii, told about an unexpected phone call from Stalin one evening in 1937. "I hear you are going about on foot," Stalin said. "That's no good. People might think what they shouldn't. I'll send you a car if yours is being repaired." And the next morning a car from the Kremlin garage arrived for Mrs. Serebrovskii's use. But two days later her

husband was arrested, taken right from the hospital.

The famous historian and publicist I. Steklov, disturbed by all the arrests, telephoned Stalin and asked for an appontment. "Of course, come on over," Stalin said, and reassured him when they met: "What's the matter with you? The Party knows and trusts you; you have nothing to worry about." Steklov returned home to his friends and family, and that very evening the NKVD [police] came for him. Naturally the first thought of his friends and family was to appeal to Stalin, who seemed unaware of what was going on. It was much easier to believe in Stalin's ignorance than in subtle perfidy. In 1938 I.A. Akulov, onetime Procurator of the USSR and later Secretary of the Central Executive Committee, fell while skating and suffered an almost fatal concussion. On Stalin's suggestion, outstanding surgeons were brought from abroad to save his life. After a long and difficult recovery, Akulov returned to work, whereupon he was arrested and shot.

In the early 1960's, Yale University psychologist Stanley Milgram devised and carried out a dramatic experiment to find out how widespread is the cruelty impulse. His research has been called the "Eichmann Experiment." Adolph Eichmann was a leading German Nazi who was arrested after World War II and charged with overseeing the extermination of millions of Jews in concentration camps. Eichmann took the standard defense of impotent persons everywhere who find it advantageous to admit to powerlessness only if caught. He pleaded not guilty and said, "I was a tool in the hands of superior powers and authorities." Dr. Milgram wanted to measure experimentally how many persons would behave in a manner similar to Eichmann.

Milgram set the stage. First, he got a cross-section of the surrounding town of New Haven, Connecticut to volunteer for an experiment. These teachers, salesmen, laborers, and clerks were told that they were part of a research project that would test the effects of punishment on learning. Secondly, each "follower," the volunteer, was placed in a room next to a person strapped into an electric chair. The follower could see the "learner," the person in the chair, through a one-way mirror. The learner was asked a series of questions by one of Milgram's associates. Each time an incorrect answer was given, the follower was instructed to give the learner an electrical shock. Each error would bring a progressively greater shock. All the while, the follower would watch the learner squirm, suffer, and cry out. In actuality, there were no shocks. The learner was an associate of Milgram who intentionally gave wrong answers according to a plan. When the supposed shocks were applied, the learner would feign pain, the greater the voltage the more intense the acting.

We would expect a high percentage of the New Haven followers to apply severe shocks to the learner. The experiment allows them to avenge the pain that they have experienced at the hands of others and permits them to share leadership with Professor Milgram. Most psychologists predicted that only a pathological fringe of 1-2% of the townspeople would be willing to apply the maximum shock and watch the learner act out extreme pain. The intellectual world was shocked by the results. Fully 65% of those average Americans, persons who presumably abhorred Eichmann's cruelty and cowardice, went all the way! New Haven was far from unique. The basic experiment was repeated in Italy, South Africa, Australia, and Germany. The level of obedience was higher than 65% in every country, reaching 85% in Germany.

Another study, involving B-52 pilots who flew combat missions in the Vietnam War, reached a complementary conclusion. Namely, it was found that pilots feel decreasing guilt for bombing people as the altitude of their jet increases. Pilots surrounded by dials, buttons, and meters were able to apply pain easily to others because of their remoteness from the suffering of their victims. In this age of intercontinental missiles, such results should be taken seriously.

Thomas Hobbes, the great theorist on violence, would not be shocked by the Milgram or B-52 studies. He argued that human life, without laws and regulations, would be a perpetual state of war, that every person would come to dread and distrust the other. An anarchistic state would permit no agriculture, industry, navigation, trade, arts, letters, or progress to exist. Everyone would live in constant fear of attack and death from human predators. Life would be solitary, nasty, brutish, and short. Hobbes went on to suggest that, in order for individuals to profit from mutual cooperation, society must regulate their behavior so as to minimize the violence that exists between them. Society should consolidate and use violence to control thieves, murderers, and other cowardly, antisocial persons.

Violence is woven into the very fabric of society. This fact can lead to life-affirming organizations, such as a prudent police force, or to life-destroying groups, such as the Spanish Inquisitors. Whether we judge the violence controlled by society's leaders as just or unjust depends primarily upon how we define "antisocial" acts.

Societies sanction violence in many ways. Amongst the oldest forms of ritualized aggression are those in which celebrants mutiliate or flog their own bodies in the name of gods. Hooded Christian penitents wind through an Italian village while raking nail-studded pads over their bare, bloody chests. They perform this ritual in the name of a loving god who will look upon them favorably for hurting themselves. In Bali, dancers draw blood by stabbing themselves with flame-shaped daggers called krisses. They do this because their leaders teach them that to do so is the wish of a malevolent deity, Queen of the Witches. Other cultures glorify violence for more practical, easily understood reasons. It is customary for a girl in the Hamar tribe of southwestern Ethiopia to taunt a boy, her prospective husband, as he whips her publicly. Her ability to endure the whipping will earn her the privilege and honor of marrying into his clan. Each of these rites echoes with the violent cry of guilt, deprivation, and frustration. In a world of healthy persons, who cooperate with each other for a common good, it is not necessary to maim oneself as part of a loyalty oath.

To summarize, human beings are born helpless. Each of us has a choice whether we remain that way or not. Some of us learn from our failures and become the best all around person that we can. Others belabor their failures and take others down with them. Most of us have awakened in the morning to a burst of self-confidence that we are masters of our life and that our past sacrifices are bearing fruit. Our affirmative mood makes it easier for us to overlook foibles in ourselves and others. Our self-esteem inspirits us to use power for altruistic ends. Impotent persons rarely experience these mornings. They are surrounded by darkness and cry out violently in order to be heard. Their impotence corrupts, and their absolute impotence corrupts absolutely.

VI
MACHIAVELLI'S PRINCE

"In our country the lie has become not just a moral category, but a pillar of the state."
— Alexander Solzhenitsyn

"I affirm that the doctrine of Machiavelli is more alive today than it was four centuries ago." and "Three cheers for war! May I be permitted to raise this cry? Three cheers for Italy's war, noble and beautiful above all, with its 500,000 dead who are our surest wealth. And three cheers for war in general."
— Mussolini

Niccolo Machiavelli admired and heralded villains This is not unusual in the history of our species. Unscrupulous persons have often marched at the head of parades. But the sixteenth century Italian was different from most followers. Namely, he articulated an extremely cynical philosophy of power which has inspirited misanthropes and has earned him immortal infamy. He and his books have been condemned vehemently for centuries, and his name has become synonymous with lying and treachery. Satan, in the eyes of many, is called Old Nick in memory of Niccolo. Nonetheless, our Earth houses hundreds of millions of leaders and followers who embrace wholeheartedly, in practice, his prescription for social advancement while denouncing, in theory, his contempt for human nature. This phenomenon, Machiavellianism, demands our attention.

Machiavelli was born in 1469 into an old Tuscan

family residing in Florence, Italy. Will Durant, in THE RENAISSANCE, tells us that Machiavelli's father was a lawyer and government bureaucrat of moderate means who had inherited a small rural villa about ten miles outside of town. As far as we know, Niccolo's childhood was undistinguished. He was educated in the humanism of his time, learned Latin but not Greek, and fed what was to become his lifelong hunger for Roman history. Student Machiavelli knew little, and apparently cared even less, for art, mathematics, medicine, or science. If he learned about Hipparchus, who mapped the constellations; Dionysisus of Thrace, who defined the parts of speech and systematized language; or Herophilus, the physiologist who demonstrated that the brain (not the heart) is the seat of intelligence, Niccolo did not spend his time writing about them. Their power to enhance humanity no more kindled his imagination than did Christopher Columbus' landing in the New World when Niccolo was twenty-three. Niccolo, from youth on, was a specialist. He had one consuming passion, the chessgame that is politics. He loved the intrigues, plots, stakes, and ego battles that absorb politicians everywhere.

While still in his twenties, the would-be Prince Machiavelli had a turn of good fortune. Lorenzo the Magnificent, a relatively mild despot and generous patron of the arts who had ruled Italy for twenty-three years, died. This event set the stage for the subsequent expulsion of the famous Medici banking family, which ruled Florence, from his hometown. This was a big break for Machiavelli, whose family had long opposed the Medici. With the Medici gone, a republic was formed.

The Republic of Florence appointed the young Machiavelli to be secretary to the Council of Ten for War, a group of magistrates responsible for the creation of diplomatic policies and the supervision of military personnel and equipment. In his initially modest role as note taker, editor, and letter writer, the aspiring diplomat was able to listen to confidential negotiations and travel throughout Italy, France, and Germany. This permitted him to practice the art of politics and, if the two can be separated, to arrange acquaintanceships for his own aggrandisement. His ability impressed Gonfalonier Piero Soderini, the leader of the Florentine government, who took on Machiavelli as his confidant. Over a period of fourteen years, Machiavelli thus advanced from passive recorder of meetings to active negotiator and was sent on missions to Countess Caterina Sforza (who outsmarted him) and to Emperor Maximilian, among others. Machiavelli, also, had the invaluable opportunity to follow the court of King Louis XII of France from chateau to chateau and to absorb, thereby, all the gossip that he could remember and use at the appropriate future dates.

Machiavelli's most notable success with the Council of Ten for War evolved out of his love of war. He had long argued that one reason Italy was a weak coalition of five powers, the Kingdom of Naples, Rome and the papal state, Venice, Florence, and Milan, was that she depended upon mercenary soldiers led by hired "condottieri", rather than upon a conscripted army of citizens under the command of another citizen, their prince. Mercenaries, as he rightly noted, could always be bought by a richer enemy. After much lobbying, Machiavelli persuaded the government to empower him to organize a militia, consisting of peasants accustomed to hardship and fear of authority, in order to advance and protect the interests of Florence's leaders. In 1508 he led this small army against the city of Pisa, which had a history of disagreements with Florence. Pisa surrendered and, when she did so, elevated Machiavelli's reputation to the greatest height he would achieve.

But victory was short-lived. In 1512 Pope Julius II, a warrior who kept Italy in turmoil while sponsoring Michelangelo and Raphael's work on St. Peter's Cathedral and the Sistine Chapel ceiling, ordered the troops of his Holy League to attack Florence and reinstate the Medici. Machiavelli's militia was ordered to defend the city, which had outraged Julius for not joining other Italian powers in the fight against France. When the well-trained mercenary army in the service of the Vatican neared Machiavelli's citizen troops, the latter ran for their lives. Florence fell, and the Medici rose.

The roof collapsed on Machiavelli. His close tie with Soderini, for whom he was a "lackey" according to Soderini's foes, was a serious liability. Other members of the chancellery were permitted to keep their jobs, but not Machiavelli. The new princes, including Lorenzo de' Medici, did not take kindly to the militia leader. They ousted him from his governmental duties without delay but did not erase him from their memories. A year later, Machiavelli was arrested on suspicion of conspiring to overthrow the state (which, of course, he denied), and was tortured with four turns of the rack. The man who dreamed of outmaneuvering the King of France, the Senate of Venice, and the pope over drunken dinners had fallen upon hard times.

It was not these relatively commonplace ups and downs of life that placed Machiavelli in history textbooks from snowy Sweden to sunbaked Brazil. Rather, his lasting impact began after his release from jail, at which time he fled prudently to his ancestral villa at San Casciano with his wife and four children. Then and there, in exile, he started to author books. Among them were MANDRAGOLA, a comedy written for the stage, and BELFAGOR ARCIDIAVOLO, a satire on the institution of marriage. But the topic he is most remembered for is politics.

Machiavelli's major work is an internationally famous treatise on princeship, a thin collection of essays entitled THE PRINCE. This book is brutally direct and unpretentious. Basically, it is a concise how-to manual, a primer for persons with the ambition and the temperament to acquire, maintain, and increase power over other people by any means necessary. Though Machiavelli wrote for those who aspire to control governments, his message is equally applicable to persons who wish to dominate families, businesses, and organizations large and small without regard to ethics. To his credit, Machiavelli kept self-censorship to a minimum and did not use the language of diplomacy to conceal his thoughts. His message is raw and provocative. Because of this, THE PRINCE has become a favorite study guide for a diverse list of kings, dictators, and intriguers who would have neither the time nor the inclination to wade through a perplexing text. King Charles V studied THE PRINCE carefully; Fuhrer Adolph Hitler kept it at his bedside; and Italian dictator Mussolini selected it as the topic for his doctoral dissertation. Henry III and Henry IV of France had it with them at their death. Bismark, Frederick of Prussia, Lenin, Richelieu, and Stalin did their homework on Machiavelli. Nobody knows how many mayors, governors, salesmen, priests, and professors have

THE PRINCE hidden in their desk drawer. In any case, THE PRINCE, often referred to as "the handbook of dictators," is a bible for many persons.

THE PRINCE, a controversial bible, has been attacked repeatedly in the last three hundred years both by humanitarians, who want more out of life than cruelty, and by hypocritical autocrats, who desire to keep their methods secret. Leaders of the Inquisition, that unholy alliance of religion and torture that stunted Europe for generations, decreed the total destruction of all of the Italian's writings except, presumably, for their personal copies. But in Machiavelli's lifetime, as is often the case with immortal works, THE PRINCE made no enemies or friends. It was ignored. This bothered Machiavelli, because he wrote the book for a very practical reason. He wanted to secure employment by flattering the leaders of Florence and by impressing his superiors that he was a perceptive thinker who could be exploited in their service. Towards this end, he dedicated his study of power to Lorenzo de' Medici, a nephew of Pope Leo X (who actually ruled Florence), with these words:

> It is customary for those who wish to gain the favour of a prince to endeavour to do so by offering him gifts of those things which they hold most precious, or in which they know him to take especial delight. In this way princes are often presented with horses, arms, cloth of gold, gems, and such-like ornaments worthy of their grandeur. In my desire, however, to offer Your Highness some humble testimony of my devotion, I have been unable to find among my possessions anything which I hold so dear or esteem so highly as that knowledge of the deeds of great men which I have acquired through a long experience of modern events and a constant study of the past.

With the utmost diligence I have long pondered and scrutinised the actions of the great, and now I offer the results to Your Highness within the compass of a small volume: and although I deem this work unworthy of Your Highness's acceptance, yet my confidence in your humanity assures me that you will receive it with favour, knowing that it is not in my power to offer you a greater gift than that of enabling you to understand in a very short time all those things which I have learnt at the cost of privation and danger in the course of many years.

The basic theme of the handbook presented to Lorenzo is simple enough: to wit, a "prince," which is to say a ruler, should be motivated by success alone. Moral or ethical considerations, judgments regarding the intrinsic value of an act, are superfluous and should be ignored. All decisions should be based on that which is opportune or politic. This amorality implies that a prince should court those vices that augment power and steer clear of those virtues that reduce power. A leader should do, Machiavelli advises, what is appropriate to transform the situation in which he finds himself into success by the quickest and most efficient route. Sometimes kindness, sometimes harshness, sometimes honesty, and sometimes deceit are the right course of action.

Imagine that a person is apprehended by the police for plotting to assassinate a prince (not so different from Machiavelli's arrest) and, furthermore, that he is condemned by the prince to hang. A humanitarian's first question should be whether the convicted person actually intended to kill the prince. Not so with Machiavelli. He considers the factual guilt or innocence of the jailed individual insignificant. The Florentine cynic is much more concerned with the public theater surrounding the hanging. He councils his prince to deliberate upon what effect a well advertised hanging will have on the public at large and upon the small minority of persons who are potential assassins. In the chapter, "In What Way Princes Must Keep Faith," he writes:

> Everybody sees what you appear to be, few feel what you are, and those few will not dare to oppose themselves to the many, who have the majesty of the state to defend them... from which there is no appeal, the end justifies the means.

The end result for every prince is to maintain the power of life and death over his subjects. Therefore, if the prince decides that it enhances his image and authority to execute a person randomly rounded up at the nearest restaurant, then he is completely justified to do so. But, Machiavelli notes, the prudent prince is obliged to do a little work to pay for the joy of hanging one of his citizens. He should labor diligently to frame the man whom he murders. That is, he should fabricate enough credible evidence so that the public is convinced of the so-called assassin's guilt. This contrived and well-publicized proof will lead the prince's followers to admire his respect for justice. This precaution will also insure that no individual who understands the prince's true motives will dare to speak for fear of being hounded by the prince's loyal servants.

Scientific truth, whereby professed beliefs and observable facts must correspond to each other, plays little, if any, role in Machiavelli's worldview. He would have us declare that $2 + 2 = 3$, when we are purchasing groceries, and that $2 + 2 = 5$, when we are selling foodstuffs, if we could find someone dumb and powerless enough for us to swindle without fear of being detected and punished. The concept of "truth" that he advocates is not only unscientific, but convoluted and self-serving to an extreme. A prince of his stamp would be candid and perceptive to admit, "The fundamental truth of the Cosmos is that I (the prince) want to dominate other people. Any talk or behavior on my part, no matter how contradictory, nonsensical, or dishonest it may be, that contributes to my authority is consistent with truth." Illogic of this variety, which is practiced commonly by princes and closely allied superstitionists, underlies much of the diplomacy that Machiavelli applauds. Thus, when we hear one of his princes declare that his slaves have "everything to live for," it is necessary to complete his line of thought. He is really announcing, "I am everything, and my slaves breathe, eat, and sleep for me. Therefore, they have everything to live for."

Machiavelli unabashedly justifies lying, censoring, and cheating. He says that whoever wants to govern people must begin with the assumption that all men are not only evil but eager to express their vicious nature whenever they can do so without fear of loss. Men, therefore, deserve to be ill-treated. If a man's nasty disposition is concealed, it is only because he lacks the proper circumstances to be cruel. The wise prince should not be fooled. He should be cautious and arrange for the fellow's true character to come forth in an environment under the prince's control. Women rank even lower in Machiavelli's eyes. We are told this, implicitly, in Machiavelli's failure to mention one kind word, in all his writings, about his wife. Explicitly, he wrote such degrading letters about prostitutes, whom he visited regularly, that even his most sympathic biographers have been unwilling to print them. Machiavelli notes that fortune is a woman, and it is necessary, if you wish to master her, to conquer her by force. It can be seen, he says, that she lets herself be overcome by the bold rather than by those who proceed coldly. Therefore, like a woman, fortune is a always a friend to the young, because they are less cautious, fiercer, and master her with greater audacity. On numerous occassions, he connects his contempt for feminine weakness [really his own, of course] with the worst elements of Christianity, which he describes in this passage from another of his books, DISCOURSES:

> The Christian religion makes us hold of small account the love of this world, and renders us more gentle. The ancients, on the contrary, found their highest delight in this world... Their religion beatified none but men crowned with worldly glory, such as leaders of armies and founders of republics; whereas our religion has rather glorified meek and contemplative men than men of action. It has placed the supreme good in humility and poorness of spirit, and in contempt for worldly things; whereas the other placed it in greatness of mind, in bodily strength, and in all that give men daring.... Thus the world has fallen a prey to the wicked, who have found men readier, for the sake of going to paradise, to submit to blows rather than to resent them....

The Florentine's preoccupation with evil, which reflects his self-image and the persons he chose to associate with, has no redeeming social value except to serve as a bad example of how to confront life. The human capacity for self- destruction does not lead Machiavelli to focus upon Leonardo da Vinci, Michaelangelo, or other life affirming contemporaries. Nor does the omnipresent wickedness of his world inspire Machiavelli to propose a nobler course of action for our species. Rather, he is content to insist that our past, present, and future is cursed by an unerasable flaw reminiscent of "orginal sin." Contemporary events, he writes, ever resemble those of preceding times. The perpetuation of gloom continues because humans were, are, and always will be motivated by the same despicable passions. We are diseased creatures, according to weary and tormented Machiavelli, and the only realistic antidote for our illness is a large injection of poison. Men can be made tolerable, he informs us, only by the organized application of force, deceit, and habit. So the prince, whom followers look to for guidance, should become expert at vile behavior. He should become a malignant actor in the theater that is life. Under the heading "Of the Things for Which Men, and Especially Princes, Are Praised or Blamed," he prescribes:

> A man who wishes to make a profession of goodness in everything must necessarily come to grief among so many who are not. Therefore it is necessary for a prince, who wishes to maintain himself, to learn how not to be good, and to use this knowledge and not use it, according to the necessity of the case.

Many historians, including Meinecke in Germany and Lord Acton in England, have referred to Machiavelli as the founder of modern political science, or as one of the fathers of modern historical analysis, for such frank and negative descriptions of humankind and politics as this quote reveal. To digress for a moment and understand why they believe this, consider the introduction to Aristotle's THE POLITICS. This book, written in the third century B.C. and read by the educated classes throughout the world for many centuries, advocated slavery and other injustices. Nonetheless, it began as follows:

> Our own observation tells us that every state is an association of persons formed with a view to some good purpose. I say 'good' because in their actions all men do in fact aim at what they think good. Clearly then, all associations aim at some good, that one which is supreme and embraces all others will have also as its aim the supreme good. That is the association which we call the State, and that type of association we call political.

Machiavelli not only thought 'good' was ludicrous but gave lessons on how to be bad. He advocates, for a start, that men learn precisely, presumably by trial and error, how much to injure others in order to optimize control over them. It must be noted, he writes in the chapter, "Of Mixed Monarchies," that men must either be caressed or annihilated. The prince should learn how to cripple people just enough that he need not fear vengeance. In other passages, Machiavelli preaches that people should be distracted with festivals; that the public should be confused intentionally; and that the prince should lie about humanity, integrity, mercy, and religion.

To compensate for this grim appraisal of humanity, Machiavelli offers us his heroes, one of whom was Pope Alexander VI. Alexander, we are told in chapter XVIII, did nothing else but deceive men, because he thought of nothing else. No man, Machiavelli proudly asserts, was better able to give assurances, or affirm things with stronger oaths, and observe them less than Alexander. This talent inspired Machiavelli to write, "But it is necessary to be able to disguise this character [the liar] well, and to be a great feigner and dissembler; and men

119

are so simple and so ready to obey present necessities, that one who deceives will always find those who allow themselves to be deceived.''

Hero number two, Agathocles, was a Silcilian who rose from the lowest and most abject social position to become the King of Syracuse. The son of a potter, Machiavelli tells us, he led a life of utmost wickedness at every stage of his career. Nevertheless, his despicable character was accompanied by such vigour of mind and body that he rose quickly through the ranks of the militia. Having decided to climb further, to become a prince, Agathocles he called together one morning the people and senate of Syracuse, as if he had to deliberate with them on important matters of state. With an agreed upon signal, he had his soldiers murder all the senators and the richest men present. After their deaths, he occupied the city and, not surprising, ruled without any civil strife. Upon this inhumane act, Machiavelli reflects:

> Some may wonder how it came about that Agathocles and others like him, could, after infinite treachery and cruelty, live secure for many years in their country and defend themselves from external enemies without being conspired against by thier subjects; although many others have, owing to their cruelty, been unable to maintain their position in times of peace, not to speak of the uncertain times of war. I believe this arises from cruelties being exploited well or badly.

From Agathocles, Machiavelli learned the calculus of pain, that cruelty should be measured like teaspoons of sugar until the perfect sweetness is found.

The third hero, Caesar Borgia, became the driving engine behind Machiavelli's philosophy, at least for a while. Borgia, six years Machiavelli's junior, was a man of action who had little use for literature or culture. Reputed to be strong enough to bend horseshoes with his bare hands, the son of Pope Alexander VI was a blond haired and bearded warrior with high ambition. This meant, for him, to become a general and lead mercenary armies to victories for the Vatican and his family. With a shrewd mind and a famous sword engraved with scenes from the life of Julius Caesar, he did exactly that. By 1502, when Machiavelli first met him at Urbino, Borgia had overthrown a dozen tyrants and had become a feared man. In particular, Borgia had stirred all Italy by capturing, strangling, and caging a group of conspirators who thought him an unworthy tyrant. Machiavelli, the theoretical ruler, was awfully inspired by these bloodthirsty deeds of a practical prince.

Borgia was a man of mystery who often worked at night and was rarely seen by day. This caused many rumors to circulate about him. One of the most common was that he and his father conspired to kill rich cardinals by placing an arsensic-based powder in their Sacramental wine at Mass. He was also said to show off his bowmanship by standing in a safe place and shooting prisoners with arrows as they ran for cover in the prison courtyard. Whether these tales were facts or fictions, it is impossible to say. But we do know that Rome considered it dangerous to be a rich cardinal and that it was widely believed that Borgia's apartment at the Vatican hosted a dinner party in which nude courtesans chased chestnuts that were thrown on the floor. Machiavelli, for his part, let none of this deter him from judging Caesar Borgia the bravest and wisest man in all Italy.

But times change, as do the sentiments of self-centered opportunists. On August 5, 1503, Alexander and

Caesar Borgia were struck, simultaneously, by malaria, which caused the pope's death on the 18th of August. The son lived, but while doctors bled him with leeches, those aristocratic enemies whom he had defeated reclaimed their lands and jockied to control who would become the new pope. On the 22nd of September, Cardinal Piccolomini (who took the name Pius III) was chosen as a compromise pope. He was friendly to Borgia, but died on the 18th of October. Soon, Cardinal Giuliano della Rovere, one of Borgia's worst enemies, was elected pope and took the name Julius II. Borgia was placed under house arrest and, true to THE PRINCE, Machiavelli switched sides. Machiavelli, who thought Christian pacifism to be ridiculous and treasonable, idolized the Borgia just weeks before. But, now, he joined the mob in denouncing Borgia as a criminal and a rebel against Christ. THE PRINCE describes the philosophy behind Machiavelli's change of heart: "...he [the prince] must have a mind disposed to adapt itself according to the wind, and as the variations of fortune dictate...."

The exiled diplomat, in addition to providing us with these masters of trickery, deception, and lies as role models, gives further advice on how to earn a reputation. First and foremost, a prince in search of a name must aim every action towards attaining fame for being great and excellent, whether he is or not. As people despise neutrality, the belligerent Italian informs us, this means that the prince should welcome constant combat. When two persons fight each other, the prince should join the battle and declare sides because, if he does not, the victor will attack him soon enough, to the joy of the victim. Winners, the Florentine reasons, will not seek friends among those who did not aid them in their time

of difficulty. But even champions must be chosen carefully. For one should never join forces with someone
stronger than oneself to injure another party. If he wins,
you are under his power, and a prince should always avoid
being under the will and pleasure of others.

The prince, during times of relative peace, should
encourage merit and reward high achievers. Citizens, for
example, should be urged to excel at commerce,
agriculture, and trade. Success in these fields will not
only keep the populace happy and preoccupied, but it will
increase the national wealth and, thereby, the tax base
for the prince. Machiavelli realized, as did the much more
successful Napoleon who read him, that one of the best
ways to keep potential rivals under control is to give them
medals. This establishes the prince as judge and the
would-be competitor as an inferior. Of course, praise for
others should be broadcast to the public. For it
demonstrates the prince's high standards and, thus, aids
his reputation.

I could give examples of Machiavelli's philosophy
for the next hundred pages. But that has been done in
essays and books for centuries. It is essential that we not
get lost in the trees debating Machiavelli's ideas about
why followers change leaders easily and quickly, why
acquired wealth has advantages over inherited wealth,
why love is a chain of obligations less binding than fear,
or why people forget the murder of their father faster than
the confiscation of their property. THE PRINCE is no
mind-boggling series of cryptograms or aphorisms. It is
simply a bitter book written by a man who wanted
desperately, but failed, to release his rage towards
humanity on a large scale, to become a prince. This cannot be denied by anyone aware of his biography.

Machiavelli even confessed such in an often quoted letter to his friend Vettori, who was Florence's ambassador to Rome. He begins by discussing how he spends a typical day and ends by revealing his feelings at the time that he wrote the book.

> In the afternoon I go back to the inn. There I generally find the host, a butcher, a miller, and a couple of brickmakers. I mix with these boors the whole day, playing at cricca and tric trac, which games give rise to a thousand quarrels and much exhange of bad language; and we generally wrangle over farthings, and our shouts can be heard in San Casciano town. Steeped in this degradation my wits grow moldy, and I vent my rage at the indignity of fate...

> At nightfall I return home and seek my writing room; and divesting myself on its threshold of my rustic garments, stained with mud and mire, I assume courtly attire; and thus suitably clothed, I enter within the ancient courts of ancient men, by whom, being cordially welcomed, I am fed with the food that alone is mine, and for which I was born, and am not ashamed to hold discourse with them and inquire the motives of their actions; and these men in their humanity reply to me; and for the space of four hours I feel no weariness, remember no trouble, no longer fear poverty, no longer dread death; my whole being is absorbed in them. And since Dante says that there could be no science without retaining that which is heard, I have recorded that which I have acquired from the conversation of these worthies, and have composed a pamphlet, THE PRINCE, in which I plunge as deeply as I can into cogitations upon this subject, discussing the nature of princedom, of how many species it consists, how these are to be acquired, how they are maintained, why they are lost; and if you ever cared for any of my scribbles,

this one ought not to displease you. And it should be especially welcome to a new prince; for which I dedicate it to his Magnificence, Giuliano.

Many commentators on Machiavelli have tried to ignore or downplay the underlying spirit of impotence and anger that is crystal clear in passages such as the preceding. The French writer Rousseau chose to admire Machiavelli because the Italian advanced the idea that the vitality of a political organization necessitates a collective mandate which is greater than the summation of individuals who make up the political unit. Jacobins, during the French Revolution, tried to convince themselves and others that THE PRINCE was a satire written by a man who opposed its major themes. Nineteeth century European readers, exemplified by German historian Leopold von Ranke, believed that, because THE PRINCE urges the liberation of Italy from foreign rulers, Machiavelli advocated only the temporary violation of human rights in the service of a higher goal. Machiavelli, for this group, was a respectable prophet for nationalism. Philosopher Hegel, who believed the "absolute Idea" (the goal of all history) was symbolized by the Prussian state, wrote this of the Florentine hater of mankind:

THE PRINCE has often been cast aside with horror as containing maxims of the most revolting tyranny; yet it was Machiavelli's high sense of necessity of constituting a state which caused him to lay down the principles on which alone states could be formed under the circumstances. The isolated lords and lordships had to be entirely suppressed; and though our idea of Freedom is incompatible with the means which he proposes... including, as these do, the most reckless violence, all

125

kinds of deception, murder, and the like; yet we must confess that the despots who had to be subdued were assailable in no other way.

Hegel's embarrassing apology, which praises Machiavelli's "high sense of necessity of constituting a state", swings the door wide open for the continuing reckless violence that has scarred human history. Machiavelli's point is that princes, in the name of creating states but actually in their own self-interest, should deceive peoples and lead them into war. All princes have as their reason for being the necessity of creating larger political units by any means necessary. Machiavelli writes, in the chapter "The Duties of a Prince with Regard to the Militia":

> A prince should therefore have no other aim or thought, nor take up any other thing for his study, but war and its organization and discipline, for that is the only art that is necessary to one who commands, and it is of such virtue that it not only maintains those who are born princes, but often enables men of private fortune to attain to that rank.

If there were not lords in Italy to fight, Machiavelli's prince would CREATE THEM elsewhere!

Those who seek to dilute and to justify Machiavelli either want to rationalize their own distaste for humanity without saying so forthrightly, or they are naive. They fall victim to advice given by Christian Gauss, an American historian, who ended his introduction to an edition of THE PRINCE with these words: "Its [the book's] bitterness is the result of his failure in his time. The modern reader cannot afford to allow this to blind them to what it contains which is still valid for our own day."

Gauss's statement completely overlooks the central attraction of Machiavelli's book. THE PRINCE is read and acted upon by countless persons not in spite of its bitterness but because it is bitter. The manual consoles persons in every generation for whom life is an acrid, biting experience that they are not alone. The book invigorates persons who manipulate the weakness in others because they lack the courage, industry, and talent to optimize the strength of others. THE PRINCE, as with all immortal books, talks to persons throughout the ages because it is relevant to their daily emotions, beliefs, and actions.

In recent years, we have witnessed many public Machiavellians at work. The White House, under the reign of President Richard Nixon, housed intrigues right off the darkest, most sinister pages of THE PRINCE. Nixon, a morbidly distrustful, insecure, and antisocial person, appointed Harvard professor Henry Kissinger, an authority on national intelligence agencies and secrecy, to the position of Secretary of State. Kissinger, obsessed with the lust for power (the "ultimate aphrodisiac" as he allegedly called it) and ruthlessly determined to destroy rivals, was a perfect match. These two men, who disliked each other as they do humanity at large, played upon each other's weaknesses at every opportunity. Kissinger flattered Nixon's fragile ego, and Nixon reciprocated by needling and coaxing Kissinger.

Together, between 1969 and 1972, they ordered the bombing of Cambodia, plotted the overthrow of democratically elected President Allende in Chile, befriended Greek military tyrants, and generally preferred sadistic rulers to democratic regimes. This last point was obvious to intelligent Americans, as neither Nixon nor Kissinger could tolerate criticism from the public, employees, Congress, the press, or universities. In time, mainly due to the Watergate scandal, the average American was able to comprehend the tip of the iceberg of deceit.

It is tempting, but self-deceiving, to condemn a few publicly recognized Machiavellians and to assure ourselves that the remainder of humanity is purer for doing so. Millions of truck drivers, housewifes, lawyers, teachers, and salesmen are required to elevate Nixon from just another Los Angeles lawyer into a position of national leadership. For years, Nixon was a hero to upwards of one hundred million Americans who saw in him their own reflection. This is not surprising. Whoever wishes to lead the masses, must follow the mob. And, when Nixon is seen without the fanfare, he is a rather ordinary person. He admitted such implicitly when one of his candidates for the United States Supreme Court was attacked for being a mediocre jurist. Nixon responded, with more than a little irony, that there are many mediocre citizens who deserve mediocre representation.

Princedoms come in all sizes. And, while it sells books and makes good gossip to talk about famous princes, there are many princes in all walks of life. Uneducated chefs can be every bit as manipulative and conspiratorial as leaders of business, education, and government. Whoever has not watched the intrigues between men and women, played for very high stakes, is innocent of adulthood. Machiavelli's self-serving logic appeals to persons of all ambitions, whether or not they have heard his name. This is because Machiavelli speaks to the dark side of the human psyche. He flames our weaknesses and seduces many among us. The world is full of individuals who fail at a long series of tests and who hunger to be a prince (or princess) in their home (their castle) if nowhere else. They long, somewhere, to be waited upon, deferred to, and obeyed.

So far, I have provided an overview of THE PRINCE in the terminology of its author. This leaves me with a disagreeable taste in my mouth, in part because Machiavellianism is such an inherently sleazy subject matter. It is also tiresome to speak in his language, because his voice is so negative that any criticism of him inevitably echoes part of his maliciousness. Machiavelli enjoys combat in the gutter of human emotions, and whoever stays in his trench long enough will catch some of his contagious disease. This, of course, is the Florentine's desire.

It is far healthier to rise above his forum and to construct an affirmative philosophy of power. Thus, I shall offer the Affirman to defeat his Prince!

VII
BEHOLD THE AFFIRMAN!

"We are here to make affirmation of progress, ... to felicitate the noble effort of people, industry, science, the valiant march in advance, the toil to cement human concord."

—Victor Hugo

"Affirmen take intense delight in existence because we honor the Cosmos, our home."

—AFFIRMIST MANIFESTO

There are two radically inharmonious methods to attain sociological power: to oppress others, who follow in fear and to uplift others, who follow in gratitude. The former path, dark and well traveled, forms the Machiavellian prince. The second road, light and spacious, creates the Bacardian affirman. The Italian cynic has had his say. It is time for fresh air. Behold, I offer you the affirman!

The affirman's arena is much larger than the prince's stage.

Picture a cosmic fireball whirling for eons and then cooling. In our infinitesimal region of the universe, a giant hydrogen cloud sits quietly. Thousands of millenia watch unnamed stars come and go. The sun and the Earth are formed, and our planet's crust begins to warm. For the Earth's first billion years, the sun is an infant radiating only half the energy that it will generate later when humans began their climb. As the air, land, and sea absorb more sunlight, reptiles begin to flourish. Still, there are no humans. Our species emerges slowly and quietly. One million years ago, our brains were expanding almost unmeasurably. Five hundred thousand years ago, our gray matter was growing at the rate of ten cubic inches per hundred thousand years. No organ has been known to evolve so quickly. In that distant placetime, a nameless person picked up a stick or rock and fashioned the first tool. That individual, who added power to our species, was an affirman.

The Cosmos is a boundless repository for the collection, exhibition, and investigation of artistic, historic, and scientific phenomena. The universe is the Smithsonian Museum in Washington and the Louvre Museum in Paris expanded beyond our imagination. Space is a monster of energy without beginning or end. It is a colossal network of power relations in which the fundamental physical forces (nuclear, gravitational, etc.) strive for superiority. The Cosmos is an eternally turbulent laboratory that does not extend itself, but only transforms itself. It is forever self-creating and endlessly self-destroying without a goal, as the coldest, most rigid regions dance with the hottest, most turbulent sections.

Billions of galaxies surround us, and countless solar systems rotate around stars similar to our sun. If only one planet has an atmosphere conducive to life, we are not alone in the Cosmos. As the human species has existed but for a blink in astronomical time, it is probable that life elsewhere is evolved beyond the comprehension of the most visionary persons. Perhaps a super civilization has been glancing at Earth for millions of years, just as we observe bacteria cultures. Perchance we are an inferior creature living under the whim of noble, thoroughbred species that have us caged somewhere in galactic zoos. Homo sapiens has no way of knowing whether such superbeings exist and, in particular, whether we are that animal. But we must find out, and the affirman will lead us towards that goal. If no life exists elsewhere, humans face the equally mind-boggling fact that we are alone. Life elsewhere or not, our evolution has just begun. We have billions of years before our sun becomes a red giant and engulfs the Earth. This vast stretch of time is available for us to surpass ourselves, just as we have outgrown our primitive ancestors.

Our species is a child of the Cosmos. Our galactic genealogy, however, remains hidden to even the greatest minds among us. Confucius, Homer, Darwin and Einstein used different vocabularies to express their hunches, and ultimate ignorance, about our origins. That is the bad news. The good news is that these hardy individuals cleared two valuable trails: science, the poetry of the intellect, and poetry, the science of the passions. The affirman employs both science and poetry to explore, test, and articulate the Cosmos. The affirman appreciates both the calculus of Newton and the nuance of Shakespeare. Science and poetry are by far the most fertile languages that mankind has created. They are much richer than the prince's political rhetoric.

The affirman aids and celebrates mankind's continuing evolution. It is a safe bet that our prehistoric ancestors were in awe of clouds. Surely, they were mystified by how white billowy clouds turn black and rain. Their great grandchildren attributed the mystery of precipitation to rain gods and, finally after many centuries, their great grandchildren discovered water vapor. These three man-

133

ners of seeing clouds reflect the exhilarating transition from preliterate ignorance, to learned superstition, to verifiable knowledge. The affirman is a positive individual who applauds this progressive chain. He, or she, values the utilization of fire, the invention of agriculture, the beginning of language, the revolution of Copernicus, the shift from political tyranny to democracy, the landing of men on the moon, and each rung on the ladder upon which our species climbs out of ignorance and superstition. These advancements are not miracles, but the result of human courage, labor, and talent. To cherish these gifts is one responsibility of being fully human.

We live in a distinguished age. Our century has shifted from whale blubber, to coal, to petroleum, to liquid oxygen fuels. Alexander Fleming has discovered penicillin, Gregory Pincus has produced oral contraceptive pills, Max Planck has introduced quantum mechanics, and William Shockley has invented the transistor. Our children, once terrified of clouds, can now make them routinely in high school chemistry classes. The affirman has scaled enormous heights since our ancestors crouched around campfires to keep warm and to frighten wolves. But the affirman is not complacent. He is knocking on the door of provocative revolutions for which computerization, genetic engineering, nuclear fusion, and space exploration are guideposts. These great upheavals, which will appear laughably primitive to future generations, are made possible by the affirman. Our spectacular epoch will be remembered for these advances, not for the devastating wars that princes have evoked since people lived in caves.

The affirmative dialogue among scientists, engineers, inventors, and nature frightens many persons. Their fear is easy to explain. In the highly technological United States, 95% of the adult population knows little more about biology, chemistry, or physics than their counterparts in rural Africa. These Americans cannot speak the universal language that governs the Space Age, mathematics, just as their ancestors could not speak the language that ruled the Middle Ages, Latin. Our electronic culture is overcrowded with persons who watch televisions, board airplanes, and use telephones without having any idea whatsoever how these devices work. Imagine living in an agricultural society and knowing nothing about shovels, picks, and hoes. Fear of the Space Age relfects nothing more or less than a crisis in our educational system.

Revolutionary eras, such as our own, strain most persons. The standards for success and, indeed, the rules for survival are in flux. At the turn of this century, the majority of Americans resided in rural areas and farmed their basic foodstuffs. Success meant understanding and cooperating with spring rains, summer crops, fall harvests, and winter storms. Today, Americans are crammed into cities. Nature is seen, if at all, as spring flowers combatting smog and summer skies peaking through neon lights. Success means bulldozing corner lots and building highrise apartment complexes. Nature is far removed from most of our fellow citizens. At best, our neighbors spend a week each year in Yellowstone National Park with crowds of other persons. This alienation from nature and science leaves modern man in limbo, rootless, and uncomprehending.

Traditional attitudes about the Cosmos are being altered drastically. Children can monitor satellites, and adults can purchase artificial hearts. The penetrating eyes of atomic accelerators, electron microscopes, and radio

135

telescopes reveal subatomic particles, biological organisms, and astronomical bodies that bewilder our brightest citizens. It is little wonder that hundreds of millions of persons, who are emotionally bound to worldviews determined by mass media advertisers are shaken by great leaps forward. It is no surprise that princes, such as President Ronald Reagan (who admits knowing less about electronics than kindergarten students) can terrorize these people with his belief that the Space Age means atomic bombs and guided missiles. The same prince Reagan, after years of breathing smog in Los Angeles, proclaimed that trees are a greater source of pollution than automobiles!

The affirman reveres past attainments and urges future achievements. He cheers persons who add to humanity. He esteems all contributors, be they more powerful, as talented, or less skilled than himself. He rises above jealousy and snobbery. No earthly insight frightens the affirman, who holds that even the most gifted humans have merely touched the cosmic riddles. Our predecessors, who preferred heroes' truths to princes' lies, toiled to understand the universe, just as farmers till the soil to bring forth sustenance. So too, the affirman affirms truth and, by standing on the shoulders of courage and genius, climbs heroically within a Cosmos indifferent to his existence. The affirman appreciates, studies, and augments what he has inherited from the best laborers who have walked the Earth.

Persons can become wise in varing areas and degrees. They can find a meaningful place under the sun by observing and understanding other people and their environment. Sagacity can be expressed in essays, lectures, letters, music, novels, paintings, poems, casual conversation, and quiet walks in the forest. Victor Hugo's tribute to Voltaire on the one hundredth anniversary of his death and Emile Zola's courtroom defense of the falsely accused French Jew, Alfred Dreyfus, are lasting examples of affirmist speeches. Our literature includes Goethe's FAUST, Hesse's THE GLASS BEAD GAME, Rabelais' GARGANTUA AND PANTAGRUEL, and Whitman's LEAVES OF GRASS. The wisdom of these works is within grasp of all curious, persistent, and courageous persons. Insight is not, as princes' claim, the private property of persons honored by the state.

The affirman welcomes lucidity. He clarifies the perplexities of existence, rather than concocting muddles. He prefers crisp language to jargon. Unlike a prince, he stands on a mountain and sees beyond the valley of mental gymnastics and double talk. Talk for the sake of talk is abstract and a waste of energy. Life has too many challenges to sit around exercising one's vocal chords. The affirman converses only as a prelude to action. Historian Arnold Toynbee noted that a life which does not go into action is a failure; and this is just as true of a prophet's, a poet's, or a scholar's life as it is true of "man of action's" life.

Affirmative action requires intelligence. Intelligence, the capacity of humans to meet effectively, through the employment of perception, memory, imagination, and conceptual thinking, the practical and theoretical problems which challenge them, is the essence of humanity. Intelligence distinguishes us from bees and fleas, animals that share much with us on the level of molecular biology.

Esteem for intelligence is far from universal. Many parents, teachers, and employers are displeased by persons with an abundance of thinking power. These authority figures realize that thinking persons do not blindly follow them. On a larger scale of hostility against intelligence, theologians council that all men are born into sin, while psychiatrists preach that all men are born into illness. Many persons believe that to raise their arm at the proper angle and to utter a sacred slogan is more notable than depth of mind. These persons, reminiscent of termites that flex their antenna in the presence of their queen, are victims of blind obedience to doctrines that mankind is either sinful or sick. The affirman clearly and emphatically renounces these negations of mankind, these scoffs that erode the foundation for honor and dignity. Humans are born into a sapient form of life, a tribute to billions of years of biological adaptation. Sin and sickness characterizes those persons who oppose the grandeur of our intelligent heritage.

Man's intelligence is rooted in sensuality. We have evolved further than other animals because our burgeoning memory of sensual trials and errors is more developed than theirs. We have learned to master fire by responding to burnt fingers and taught ourselves to grind lens by reacting to sore eyes. And we have gone much further. We can see bateria with microscopes, touch Mars' soil with robots, and hear underground rock movement with seismographs. Applied intelligence has given us the power to build upon our senses. Conversely, as the technology of our species heightens, we may discover new senses within our bodies. Prolonged exposure to zero gravity space has already suggested a sixth sense, the power of the inner ear to establish equilibrium. This faculty may have escaped us for a million years because Earth's gravity has permitted us to distinguish "up" from "down."

138

The historical advance of our intellect and senses testifies to human genius. The affirman salutes this genius for two vital reasons. First, particular geniuses such as Homer, Balzac, and Madame Curie are consummate teachers from whom all persons can learn about themselves and the universe. They, not Machiavellian tyrants, are our heroes. Secondly, mankind possesses a genius that separates us from other animals. Every person has skills far beyond those of monkeys and dogs. To praise genius is, thus, to extol the most powerful human beings and to commend the power common to all humans. The legacy of genius is the backbone of civilization. In practice, the affirman admires the pursuit of excellence in art, athletics, carpentry, character, conversation, cookery, and all life affirming activities.

Persons have defined "genius" in many ways. Plato associated it with enthusiasm and divinity, because its orginality is comparable with the creation of the gods. Leonardo da Vinci counselled artists that genius was the ability to comprehend nature, not to imitate traditional masters. Descartes employed the word to mean an unusual capacity to discover the truth, while Kant defined genius as a favorable mixture of creative spirit, judgment, sensibility, and taste. Thomas Edison called it one per cent inspiration and ninety-nine percent perspiration.

The affirman believes that genius is the most personal, enduring affirmation of life. Humans are a rapidly ascending animal and, unlike frogs, we are not content to sit in the mud and eat flies for millions of years. Our ambition is to exercise power, to mold the future by overcoming the limitations of the present. This will to power pushed Beethoven to make greater demands upon musicians than his predecessors and sparked Hume to awaken fellow thinkers from dogmatic slumber. Everyone participates in the family of genius when he climbs above the prejudices of his birthplace.

Outgrowths of genius surround us. Our automobile travels back to Henry Ford, our telephone recalls Alexander Graham Bell, and this printed page documents Johann Gutenberg. The automobile, telephone, and printing press have given birth to innumerable social values and institutions. These inventions have far outlived their inventors. Genius is nothing more than the ability to beget immortal events, ideas, or works of art. This is not surprising. The word "genius" is derived from the Latin verb "gignere," which may be translated to mean "to beget." The family of man does indeed have a Father. That Father is genius.

No human can select his biological parents. Everyone has, however, the freedom and obligation to help chose who will father and mother the future. This commitment is profound because the affirman will always promote the Thomas Edisons at the expense of the Genghis Khans, the creators instead of the destroyers. The prince mocks great persons and calls the affirman naive and elitist for praising positive heroes rather than manipulative leaders. The Machiavellian condemns us for namedropping geniuses. His complaints are a smokescreen. The prince resents bitterly our positive assertion that many persons are superior to him. The prince believes that man's purpose is to conform and, by kneeling on fright and mediocrity, to stagnate in a Cosmos that echoes his prejudices. All Hitlers become rulers by standing of the shoulders of cheering mobs of would-be princes. Much is known about a person once we hear whom he reveres, and those who negate the genius of mankind are despairing voices of death. The affirman stands on mountains above the naysayers and speaks William Blake's words for all to hear: "When thou seest an Eagle, thou seest a portion of Genius; lift up thy head!"

All the millions of life forms must develop the power to overcome misfortune. The person who cannot deal with the loss of friends will break emotionally, just as the palm tree that cannot sway in a hurricane will snap. Human puissance is not an abstract psychological state related to greed, insecurity, or socialization. Rather, our power-urge is as practical as gravity. Without power, we fall as certainly as an apple jarred loose from a tree.

Though the Earth permits us to live, it is indifferent to our existence. The world owes us nothing; it was here first. Playwright Eugene O'Neill put it this way, "You may be important but your life's not. There's millions of it born every second.... And it's not sacred - only the you inside is. The rest is earth." Perhaps, humanity will cease to exist because of a nuclear war, an incurable plague, or a huge meteor collision. The once mighty dinosaurs vanished and left only their bones. If our species, which is now endangered by princes who control nuclear weapons, becomes extinct, the Earth will continue to revolve around the sun and rotate upon its axis. Spaceship Earth will not weep for us. Cosmic indifference bestows upon us the honor and duty to be self-reliant, to improve our small region of the Cosmos.

The affirman and the prince are animals. Bacardians and Machiavellians, for all their differences, have similarities. First and foremost, each of them eats, breathes, and organizes in order to survive. Each of them resides amidst humans and other species. Each of them, finally, gives and takes energy from his environment. All animals belong to an ecosystem, a natural arena in which fauna, flora, and nonliving substances interact with each other. These intercourses produce a stable system in which an individual animal lives and dies. A closer look at ecosystems will reveal the sociological role played by the affirman and the prince.

A common ecosystem is a backyard pond. The major nonliving portion of the pond is water, the catalyst for all life on Earth. This liquid contains many nonliving substances, including dissolved gases such as carbon dioxide, soluble salts such as sodium phosphate, and chemical elements such as calcium. The living part of the pond consists of green plants, which transform gases, salts, and elements into living cells; microscopic plants, which serve as food for animals; insects and fish, which eat smaller organisms; and bacteria and fungi, which decompose dead cells into materials that can be utilized by plants. Each ingredient in the pond contributes to the overall life of the ecosystem in specific ways. Each region of the pond, be it a cool deep valley or a sunny shallow pool, affects every other section of the ecosystem.

Animals within an ecosystem may be friendly, hostile, or indifferent towards other classes or species of animals. My neighbors, for example, are generally kind to dogs, hostile to ants, and indifferent to earthworms. Animals, also, have diverse reactions to animals like themselves. Frogs can be amicable, belligerent, or unconcerned towards other frogs, as can persons towards their fellow humans.

Every ecosystem has two major power bonds amongst its member plants and animals. If two species benefit from the existence of each other and cannot survive without the other, a biological relationship called "mutualism" ex-

142

ists. Mutualistic power occurs between termites and their intestinal microorganisms. Termites can chew and swallow wood but they lack the protein catalyst to digest wood. Fortunately for these tiny insects, termites' intestines house single-celled animals that have the chemical ability to convert the cellulose found in wood into sugar. The microscopic animals consume some of this sugar for their own survival, and the surplus is available for the termites. Termites cannot survive without these small creatures. In turn, the protozoa profit because they are supplied with a regular meal of cellulose and a safe environment. If taken outside the termites' intestines, they will die. Both organisms, the termites and the protozoa, act amicably towards each other. They exercise power constructively.

Power of the second type is destructive. If one species harms another species but cannot live without the other, a biological relationship called "parasitism" exists. Parasitic power occurs when a plant or animal, a parasite, obtains nourishment from another organism, a host, without giving the host anything of value in return. Mistletoe is a parasite. This white berried evergreen grows roots into apple or apricot trees in search of food. Once the mistletoe has eaten, it injects waste products into the tree. Sometimes the mistletoe merely weakens its hosts; sometimes it kills the trees. Many parasites disease their host by releasing toxic wastes, and most plant diseases are caused by parasitic fungi. Normally, parasites have specific tastes and favor only one or two species of hosts. The infamous mosquito is an exception. It extracts blood from many species in addition to our own. In all cases, the parasite/host relationship is one-sided and, if we may apply the term to nonhuman life, exploitive.

Human society is a complex ecosystem in which persons relate with minerals, plants, and other animals. Societies and customs are so diverse that virtually any behavior found among flora and fauna has a human parallel. Ants enslave aphids, just as farmers domesticate sheep; sparrows gang up on raiding hawks, just as police surround bank robbers; and redwood trees shade ferns, just as gardeners protect fragile flowers. Our society houses the same mutualistic and parasitic powers as do simpler ecosystems. Some of us are enormously valuable to our species. Everyone benefits from our mutualistic power. Others of us are walking disaster areas. We cause misery to everyone we encounter. The gulf between human mutualists and parasites is truly amazing. Mark Twain was bold enough to observe that there are greater differences between humans than between people and apes.

Some people control the human ecosystem more vigorously than others. This fact is undeniable. No reasonable person can deny that Julius Caesar, the famous Roman military and political leader, had a greater impact on the 1st century B.C. than did his blacksmith. Caesar was effective. He had the ability to make events happen according to his plans. But his capacity to direct men and resources is only one half of his story. The more important half is whether Caesar was an affirman or a prince, a mutualist or a parasite. We should ask the same question about Caesar's blacksmith, because affirmen and princes are found everywhere on the sociological pyramid. But, practically speaking, we must overlook the blacksmith. History books tell us nothing about him.

Julius Caesar descended from an old patrician family. At the age of forty-two, after years of being an unscrupulous politician and a reckless rake, Caesar was appointed the governor of three Roman provinces. This governorship gave him control over what is now northern Italy, the coast of Yugoslavia, the southern coast of France, and about twenty thousand soldiers. For the next seven years, godlike Caesar inspired his troops to destroy, plunder, rape, and kill the inhabitants of present day France and Belgium, along with portions of Switzerland, Germany, and Holland. He conquered these lands, known then as Gaul, and built a formidable political base.

Many scholars judge Caesar's slaughter of Gaul a praiseworthy accomplishment. These historians are impressed that Gaul adopted Roman law, language and religion, that Gaul stayed under Roman rule for five centuries, and that Romanized Gaul protected Italy from northerly attacks. Clearly, Caesar was an extraordinary person. Few men have been able to earn the hatred of an infighting aristocracy, by undermining their privileges and seducing their wives, and live to tell about it. Fewer persons still have lorded over such a large geographical territory. The competition to be prince among princes can be literally cutthroat. Yet, something obvious is missing in armchair praise for Caesar; namely, the death cry of his enemies and followers. History textbook writers are usually sedentary individuals. Few of them experience the nausea of war that led William Sherman, the American Union general, to write to his wife, "I begin to regard the death and mangling of a couple thousand men as a small affair, a kind of morning dash - and it may be well that we become so hardened." Too often, historians show little, if any, concern for those nameless persons who had their arms hacked off and their characters assassinated by Caesar's road to power.

Caesar is no mystery to affirmists. The Roman tyrant

was a parasite in the human ecosystem. His vanity and glory were at the direct expense of other humans. He took from people and, when they had nothing left to give, killed them. To proclaim Caesar, or any other Machiavellian, a great human being is to tell our species a Big Lie every bit as bold and outrageous as Hitler's claim that there is a superior race. Caesar was a princely leader, but he was no affirmist hero. While the affirman encourages good health, meaningful employment, economic security, loyal friendship, community recognition, sexual pleasure, free speech, intellectual stimulation, cultural enjoyment, and a sense of beauty, Caesar guarded these enjoyable values closely. For his followers, Caesar served wartime nightmares and peacetime intrigues. Like mistletoe, he fed on his environment.

The prince is an obsessive consumer. His hunger for mansions, servants, mistresses, cheering crowds, human sacrifices, or precious metals is insatiable. In the 1780's, despite its vast authority, King Louis XVI's monarchy faced bankruptcy. His government was unable, or unwilling, to erase its debts with inflation or taxation. This monetary crisis did not cause Louis to curb his extravagant tastes at his Versailles palace any more than mistletoe eats less in order to aid an ailing Oak tree. In desperation, Louis summoned the leading French nobles together in the Assembly of Notables in 1787 and asked them to surrender their tax privileges. Thus, the chief prince pleaded with the lesser princes to give him more of their parasitic power. When the aristocrats refused, the stage was set for the French Revolution. Louis, a chubby and stupid man, would rather risk loss of his property and his life than moderate his consumption. The idea that Louis and his aristocrats should actually produce what they consumed was foreign to their mindset.

The affirman is a producer. In 1787, while King Louis was wasting social resources at Versailles, the Scottish inventor, James Watt, was creating social wealth. Watt was helping create the Industrial Revolution. As early as 1712, Thomas Newcomen had invented a steam engine that was capable of pumping water out of coal mines. But Newcomen's device was not very practical. Watt made big improvements by inventing a separate condensing chamber, in 1769, and by converting the steam energy into rotary motion with gears, in 1781. These breakthroughs increased the efficiency of the steam engine by at least threefold and gave the machine great industrial utility. With business partner Matthew Boulton, affirman Watt started manufacturing these steam engines.

The steam engine made a truly affirmative impact on our species. For thousands of years, our species' main source of energy had been human muscles. Most people were little more than beasts of burden, who exhausted themselves in fields and mines like so many oxen and horses. The energy available to humanity, dependent upon biceps and triceps, was severely limited. Watt's genius changed all this. The Scot's practical engine provided theretofore undreamed of energy to run factories, dig wells, and irrigate fields. In addition, Watt set the stage for the Marquis de Jouffroy d'Abbans and Richard Trevithick to build a steam-powered boat and locomotive, respectively. These later inventions led to steamboats and railroads, which revolutionized transportation and made the Earth a smaller planet.

Humankind has much more energy now than in Watt's day. And our species is just beginning to tap nature's power. The famous equation, "$E = mc^2$," from

Einstein's special theory of relativity permits us to calculate the quantity of energy, E, that is released when a piece of matter, m, is converted totally into energy. Because the speed of light, c (186,000 miles per second), multiplied times itself is an astronomically huge number, tiny volumes of matter can set free enormous quantities of energy under the proper conditions. A few gallons of sea water may someday provide clean nuclear (fusion) power to light a city. Solar energy (which is noneother than nuclear fusion in our sun), also, has tremendous potential. Astrophysicists have calculated that a one hour storm on the sun can generate the entire electrical power consumption of the United States for over a million years at this nation's present level of use. The sun's energy is stored in hydrogen atoms, the simplest and smallest atoms. These atoms are, along with oxygen, the building blocks of water.

Two physical laws regarding energy are germane to our study of power: the first and the second laws of thermodyamics. The first law affirms that the total mass-energy of the Cosmos is constant. There is nothing ''a priori'' or ''sacred'' about this assertion. The first law has credibility for one and only one reason: to wit, no human has demonstrated an exception to this rule. If any one does, that individual will not only win the Nobel Prize but will shake the very foundations of the learned world.

Matter-energy is neither created nor destroyed, although the form it assumes is determined by environment. Physically, a book can be submerged in liquid nitrogen until it is brittle and shatters under hammer blows. Most persons would say the frozen book has low energy. The same book, when ignited by a match, can warm a person's hands on a cold day and appears more

148

energetic than its frozen counterpart. Suppose we could transport the book into the vicinity of a powerful gravitational field, perhaps a collapsed star. The star could accelerate the book towards it with such force that, upon impact with the surface of the dead star, the hardback would explode with the ferocity of a hydrogen bomb. Sociologically, a book can motivate millions of persons in one environment and collect dust in another culture. The Iranian prophet Zoroaster, who lived in the 6th century B.C., authored GATHAS, the oldest section of the sacred scriptures of the Avesta. The GATHAS energized the Zoroastrian religion, which has endured for more than 2,500 years. Today, there are more than 100,000 adherents, mainly around Bombay, India, where they are called Parsees. The GATHAS, if written today in San Francisco, would receive countless rejection notes from publishers on the grounds that "There is no audience for this book."

The constancy of total mass-energy has practical import to both the prince and the affirman. The first law means that nothing in life is without a price and that one gets out of life only what one puts into life. The prince speaks to himself thusly, "There is only a fixed amount of power (energy) to go around, and I want it! Therefore, I must crush anyone who gets in my way. The passive masses, once they see my victories, will be afraid to disobey me." The affirman reasons, "Society is operating at too low of an energy level, because it lacks ideas and direction. I can achieve power by converting persons' latent energy into usable energy. People will follow me because I offer what they need." The affirman starts with an empty lot alongside a highway and builds a computer company by uniting the productive skills of electrical engineers, accountants, salespersons, and technicians with the consumer tastes of the public. The prince comes along, after the company is successful, and threatens the affirman with higher taxes, unfavorable zoning laws, and labor problems unless the latter bribes the prince in one form or another.

The second law of thermodynamics states that systems tend towards disorder. A crystal wine glass blown off a table is likely to shatter. The broken glass, scattered on the floor in random fashion, has less order than the un-disturbed glass. It is theoretically possible but highly unlikely that a second breeze will lift the glass slivers onto the table top and reassemble them into a wine glass. This principle of unlikely reversibility is experienced by anyone who does home repairs. Electrical sockets, light bulbs, and garage doors may stop working for many reasons, but it is relatively certain that they won't repair themselves. It requires a higher form or order, namely a person, to glue a broken glass or to rewire a bad socket.

The prince and the affirman have opposite attitudes about disorder. For the prince, chaos is a golden opportunity to seize control over the population. Machiavelli repeats this theme over and over. One of his followers, Mussolini, expressed love of disorder with these words: "You know what I think about violence. For me it is profoundly moral, more moral than compromises and transactions." A great affirmist, Goethe, wrote that when the sound and wholesome nature of man acts as an entirety, when he feels himself in the world as in a grand, beautiful, worthy and worthwhile whole, when this harmonious comfort affords him a pure, untrammeled delight: then the universe, if it could be sensible of itself, would shout for joy at having attained its goal and wonder and the pinnacle of its own essence and evolution. For what end is served by all the expenditure of suns and planets and moons, of stars and Milky Ways, of comets and nebula, of worlds evolving and passing away, if at last a happy man does not involuntarily rejoice in his existence?

Affirmen take intense delight in existence because we honor the Cosmos, our home. We are made of stardust. But can we thank the stars? Someday our skeletal structure will develop to cope with new gravitational environments, and our respiratory system will adjust to extraterrestrial atmospheres. Perhaps we shall become huge skulls supported by wiry legs and call ourselves "Homo megacephalus." None of these transformations will shake the stars or stir the galaxies, but that is not our objective. The affirman's purpose is to affirm truth and, by standing on the shoulders of courage and genius, to climb heroically within a Cosmos indifferent to his existence. This is how the affirman says thanks.

Nature favors neither the affirman nor the prince. Both have existed since the dawn of man, and both can reproduce their kind. It is your job to choose between mutualists and parasites. Join us.

VIII
THE SCALES OF JUSTICE

"Justice, sir, is the great interest of man on earth. It is the ligament which holds civilized beings and civilized nations together."

—Daniel Webster

"Justice, being destroyed, will destroy; being preserved, will preserve; it must never therefore be violated."

—Manu

About 3.6 million years ago, a volcano erupted in what is now Tanzania and coverered nearby savannahs with ash. In 1979, paleoanthropologist Mary Leakey found a footprint in that ash which, she believes, belongs to an early hominid. Had the creature died of foul play? About 15 years ago, a rocket blasted off its launching pad and into space. One of its passengers left a different footprint on a flat, dry lunar plain called the Sea of Tranquility. Will our conquest of space expand the limits of our destructive impulses? Our inspiring evolution from Africa to the Moon has been made in small steps. We have walked, oh so carefully, on a tightrope between ethics and villainy.

You walk through life. Along the road, you meet friends, relatives, and strangers. Some of these persons please you and others do not. In either case, your encounters with other humans present you with a tough choice. You must decide whether to be honest, fair, and trustworthy or to be false, mean, and disloyal. Your course of action is difficult, because you are torn by two conflicting themes. A voice preaches in one ear "Honesty is the best policy," and a second voice whispers "Nice persons finish last."

Affirmism clears the air of this stifling contradiction. We affirm that decency is not only the best policy, but that nice persons can finish first. We affirm that moral excellence adds to, rather than detracts from, achievement. This essay will applaud the just triumph of ethical persons over villains.

Let us begin with the bad news. The moral principles that most children learn are practiced rarely by adults. The high sounding Golden Rule, "Do unto others as you would have them do unto you," is judged terribly utopian by practioners of the high paying Golden Rule, "Whoever owns the gold makes the rules." The legal principles that most civics students memorize are ignored routinely by political elites. One does not have to read John Le Carre's spy novels to realize that the world's governments employ assassins, blackmailers, forgers, and burglars in the name of "national security."

Life is often harsh and unfair. Persons seldom get what they deserve. Far too often, misanthropes victimize innocent people. Amin, the former dictator of Uganda, entertained himself by watching his lackeys torture citizens who were kidnapped off the street at random. When his regime was toppled, Amin moved to Libya for a luxurious retirement. Often cruel persons are heralded as heroes. Hitler stood on the shoulders of millions of ordinary Germans who cheered his every whim. There are, of course, less energetic Amins and Hitlers in all walks of life. By contrast, I have never heard of a parade in honor of two adults who reared their children to become kind, productive citizens.

Many persons are disillusioned by the unfairness of life. Clarence Darrow, the outstanding lawyer and orator, said towards the end of his life, "The law is a horrible business. There is no such thing as justice, in or out of court." Vardis Fisher, a twentieth century educator and writer, added in his book, GOD OR CAESAR?: "Do human beings love justice? The sordid travesties in our courts year after year suggest that they love justice only for themselves. Love of ... justice... is a myth that has been created by the folk mind, and if the artist does not look behind the myth to the reality he will indeed wander amid the phantoms which he creates."

Darrow and Fisher were candid, perceptive persons. We are tempted, in the middle of the night, to share their grim summary. Clearly, those persons who injure or destroy life are many in number and speak with a loud voice. But we, life-affirming persons from all backgrounds, are too strong to be held prisoners of darkness. As Konstantin Kolenda reminds us in his excellent book, PHILOSOPHY AND LITERATURE, we welcome dawn. We embrace light.

Now the good news. Humanity has a glorious history of achieving justice against all odds. Medicine exists in spite of societies that outlawed research. Public education exists even though economies benefited from child labor. These successful battles, and future ones, are cause for rejoicing. We stand united together by the blood, sweat, and tears of countless heroically ethical kindred spirits. A great many persons make life a little better for whomever crosses their paths without being applauded by neighbors, journalists, or historians. A few affirmative persons have been immortalized. One such person is Albert Schweitzer, who noted that ethics is the maintaining of life at the highest point of development. Victor Hugo, the author of LES MISERABLES, is a second immortal. On the one hundredth anniversary of Voltaire's death, Hugo made one of the most positive speeches of all time. His final words were these:

> We are here, at this grand moment, to bow religiously before the moral law, and to say to the world, which hears France, this: "There is only one power, conscience in the service of justice."

A powerful person realizes that justice is a challenge. He or she must come conscientiously to terms with justice in two, very personal ways. First, a strong individual must affirm criteria that distinguish justice from injustice. And, second, a vigorous citizen must affirm reasons why his or her self-interest is served by ethical behavior. These are the two tasks before us. Before tackling them, it is valuable to place justice and judgment in perspective.

Justice is a purely human concept. Mars, Venus, and Earth absorb the sun's rays, but no legislature of planets allots solar energy to each revolving sphere. Horseflies and bees compete with each other for dinner but, as far as I can observe, no judge or jury passes verdicts on their table manners or consumption levels. It is a safe bet that neither a planet nor an insect has a conscience. It is equally probable that neither argues with neighbors about whether "justice" is a synonym for "law" or a broader concept closer to "fairness." Celestial bodies and six-legged creatures come and go, as poet T.S. Eliot might have noted, without speaking of Michelangelo. They neither ponder their existence nor seek external vindication for their existence. They neither reward nor punish other entities. Only humans, with all due respect to my dog, self-reflect upon their actions. This introspection enables and forces humans to judge themselves and others.

To judge is to be responsible. Impotent persons deny their judicial role in word, if not in deed. For them, to judge is to be arrogant. A recent poll discovered that 69% of America's teenagers believe in angels, 59% in extrasensory perception, and 55% in astrology. Furthermore, hundreds of thousands of American adults worship cult leaders who profess to have supernatural gifts. Helpless persons are apathetic to these facts. Powerful individuals grasp that this widespread belief in alleged paranormal phenomenon has a profound impact on our society's allocation of resources. Astrology is a billion dollar a year industry in the United States. By comparison, our space science budget during the early 1970s development of the Viking mission to Mars was only 1/4 billion dollars! Responsibility demands that persons judge whether astrology or space exploration is more valuable to society.

Many people, this is equally true among the strong and the weak, confuse mature judgments with immature prejudices. Prejudice is an opinion formed beforehand or without due examination. If a person condemns or praises astrology without any knowledge of horoscopes and sun-signs, that individual is immature and unjust. If an individual traces the historical development of the celestial "twins" astronomy and astrology, studies empirical tests of astrological predictions, and reasons that astrology is a mass popular delusion, that person is mature and just.

People discriminate in order to survive and prosper. A Chicago vagrant who can distinguish between a can of antifreeze and a bottle of wine will live longer than a wino

157

who cannot. So too, a bank officer who can tell the difference between a stable business and a likely bankruptcy will prosper better than colleagues who cannot. Much controversy surrounds discrimination, because all persons have the unquestioned right to be choosy in certain circumstances and not in others. A woman realtor may choose to date only well-educated Caucasians over six feet tall with athletic bodies. Though illiterate, squat men of many races may resent her tastes, there is nothing illegal about her dating pattern. Reasonable citizens grant each other the right to be selective, if not capricious, in their personal lives. However, if the same woman rents apartments only to well-educated Caucasian men over six feet tall with athletic bodies, she is in big trouble. Caucasian, Black, Chinese, and Hispanic men and women of all heights and educations will scream that she is violating their civil rights. The unfavored tenants will argue that their education, race, height, and body type are irrelevant criteria for renting an apartment.

What factors are relevant to justice? This question provokes much controversy. A few highly publicized baseball players earn $1,000,000 a year, while many anonymous migrant workers collect $5,000 a year. Some citizens holler that this economic inequality is perfectly just. They contend that a baseball player provides the public with 200 times more pleasure than does a farm worker and, therefore, the athlete deserves 200 times more money. Other persons cry out that this monetary discrepancy is unjust. They maintain that a person's talent to entertain us is irrelevant and that an unmarried ballplayer should be paid less than a married stoop laborer who has a wife and three children to support. Still other individuals yell foul play for a different reason. They assert that the baseball hero is talented but greedy, while they declare that the farm worker is diligent but stupid. They point out that, since everyone has strengths and weaknesses, justice dictates that everyone be paid equally. Not surprisingly, persons in each of these three camps tend to dislike members of the other two.

Justice is a volatile issue. Nonetheless, let us dare to provide three criteria that distinguish justice from injustice. Justice exists when the affirman is favored over the prince, when reciprocity is favored over hypocrisy, and when scientific evidence is favored over prejudicial opinion.

The spirit of justice prevails when the affirman has the upper hand over the prince. We have discussed both types of persons, the affirman and the prince, in previous chapters. To reiterate, the affirman believes, along with Schweitzer, that to affirm life is to deepen the will-to-live and to exalt the best in humanity. The prince believes, along with Machiavelli, that to conquer others is man's reason for living.

The line between the affirman and the prince is sharp and clear. Consider passport offices in the United States and the Soviet Union. The affirman supports Article 13 of the "Universal Declaration of Human Rights" that was adopted by the General Assembly of the United Nations on 10 December 1948. This article states: "Everyone has the right to leave any country, including his own, and to return to his country." Citizens should be issued passports upon request and permitted to cross national boundaries. The Soviet Union rejects Article 13, maintaining that life in Russia is so wonderful that nobody in his right political senses would want to leave. In American passport offices, an affirmist philosophy is pervasive. With few exceptions,

Americans can board a jet destined for almost any foreign soil. Not so in a Soviet passport bureau, where paranoid princes have the dominant voice. Many Russians who request permission to leave the country are harassed or imprisoned. With regard to passports, the United States is more just than the Soviet Union.

Princes have persecuted millions of persons over the centuries. Giordiano Bruno, an Italian Renaissance philosopher, is one victim remembered by historians. Bruno wrote that Christ was a magus and that the Egyptians' magical religion was in some respects better than Christianity. Bruno made a fatal mistake when he believed that the Vatican's princes would welcome ideas for religious and moral improvement. For his efforts, Bruno was sentenced to eight years in prison and, after serving time, was burned alive for heresy. Today, the Kremlin's princes imprison physicist Andrei Sakharov, father of the Russian hydrogen bomb, and allegedly subject him to mind altering drugs. Sakharov's "crime" was to write books such as PROGRESS, COEXISTENCE, & INTELLECTUAL FREEDOM.

Affirmen prefer to educate persons rather than to burn them. They support public schools that provide a broad education. Who would oppose such a reasonable request? The answer is easy: persons who prefer to burn books rather than to read them. Every Sunday, a famous preacher rants and raves on national television that American educators are "evil" for poisoning childrens' minds and characters. He assures millions of viewers that history, biology, mathematics, science, and foreign language classes undermine sacred morality. He pontificates that art museums, film festivals, and libraries are filled with sin and decadence. The evangelist, a mass media prince, is terrified of education. He feels imprisoned by behavior and thought that are not his own. He, a religious fundamentalist, condemns freedom of thought and action as vehemently as does his atheist revolutionary counterpart in Russia.

Princes in all geographical regions, political parties, and social classes agree with George Orwell's Big Brother that "Ignorance is Strength." For them, this slogan is sensible. Public ignorance feeds their sociological strength. They are demagogues who preach doctrines they know to be untrue to persons whom they consider to be idiots. They ask persons to mail them contributions, to vote them into office, and to sympathize with their hardships. We affirm that life itself, and people in particular, displease princes. To pander to them is an exercise in futility, because nobody can wax and wane the world according to their selfish whims. A person's time and energy are better spent pursuing knowledge than flattering princes of ignorance.

Secondly, justice exists when reciprocity is favored over hypocrisy. Let us reiterate: every person, in order to live fully and with dignity, should be encouraged to value good health, friendship, meaningful work, recreation, cultural enjoyment, sex love, educational opportunity, community recognition, freedom of speech, and a sense of beauty. Too often, society's rulers pursue these social goods privately and condemn them publicly. Victorian aristocrats traded mistresses while passing laws against adultery; Mao Tse-Tung's wife watched Hollywood movies while preaching against American degeneracy; and Roman Emperors tossed dinner guests off cliffs while condemning capricious and cruel rivals. The just person strives to minimize such double standards.

161

Confucius, who lived five hundred years before Christ, applauded reciprocity. He advised us: "Do to every man as thou would'st have him do to thee; and do not do unto another what thou would'st not have him do to thee." The Chinese sage meant that a just person takes account of the wishes of others and accords others the same respect and consideration that he would want others to give him. Followers of Confucius respected elderly members of their community, just as they expected that they would be honored in old age.

The word "golden" was used in earlier times to mean "most excellent, important, or precious." Accordingly, the principle of reciprocity has become known as the golden rule. The golden rule, in one form or another, has attained almost universal acceptance. The rule has been explicity endorsed, in word if not in deed, by countless ethical and social codes. It appears in Christianity's BIBLE, Brahmanism's MAHABHARATA, Buddhism's UDANA-VARGA, Confucianism's ANALECTS, Taoism's T'AI SHANG KAN YING P'IEN, Zorastrianism's DADISTAN-I-DINIK, and Islam's SUNNAH. Judaism's TALMUD says this about the rule: "What is hateful to you, do not do to your fellowmen. That is the entire Law; all the rest is commentary." Thomas Hobbes referred to the Golden Rule as a law of nature; John Stuart Mill called it the supreme ideal of utilitarian philosophy; and John Locke claimed it was the answer to ethics.

The golden rule, for all its popular acceptance, has critics who focus upon two flaws. The first objection is captured in George Bernard Shaw's "Do not do unto others as you would that they should do unto you. Their tastes may not be the same." Shaw and others argue that the rule assumes, erroneously, that humans have uniform

162

talents, powers, and hungers. They suggest that the rule authorizes quarrelsome persons to provoke and warriors to attack their neighbors because the former groups enjoy being provoked and attacked. We believe that reciprocity is a general behavioral guideline, not a specific prescription. Justice is served by recognizing the right of others to eat, but not by force feeding them our favorite food. The golden rule's second weakness is more serious. It advocates not only repaying good with good, but evil with evil. We believe that taking an eye for an eye and a tooth for a tooth is not the road to justice. The Mideast has witnessed too many generations of Jews, Muslims, and Christians murdering each other in the name of past crimes, just as Protestants and Catholics continue to slaughter each other in Ireland. Somewhere the vicious cycle of violence and injustice must stop. Otherwise, society contains nobody but blind, toothless citizens.

Third, justice exists when scientific evidence is favored over prejudicial opinions. Suppose someone steals a Van Gogh painting from San Francisco's Legion of Honor Museum and a suspect is arrested. The alleged thief should be considered innocent until he is proven guilty. Whether he is an affirman or a prince, his innocence or guilt should be determined only by an impartial investigation of all attainable facts surrounding the disappearance of the Van Gogh. Eyewitnesses, fingerprints, and fragments of torn clothes are examples of pertinent data. Under all conditions, the fabrication or suppression of evidence by prosecutors should be regarded as a serious crime against society as a whole, as well as against the alleged criminal.

Many persons take fair investigations for granted. So, it is worth noting that respect for objective evidence is rare. In most countries, an arrested person is assumed to be guilty and, if he cannot prove his innocence, is beaten until he confesses. Misologists rationalize such blatant injustice with words like these: "Police can spot a criminal on sight. They wouldn't arrest him for stealing a Van Gogh, unless they were positive he was a thief. Even if he didn't rob the museum, he undoubtedly stole other items that we don't know about. As for torturing him into a confession. Well, criminals are liars. You can't expect them to tell the truth without persuasion." This twisted reasoning allows countless policemen in dictatorships and democracies around the Earth to arrest their creditors, rivals, and enemies. In addition, many judges assume that unpopular minorities, be they South African blacks, French arabs, American socialists, Soviet Jews, or relatives of criminals, are guilty as charged just because of their race, religion, politics, or family.

Facts can be found only by digging beneath circumstantial evidence. Consider the following twist of events. Two men, one husky and the other emaciated, are lost in a winter storm. Covered with snow, these weary and hungry persons stumble across a mountain cabin. They knock, but nobody answers. They force their way inside and search for food. The shelves contain only one small can of tuna. Immediately, the large man shoves the skinny fellow aside, opens the can with his hunting knife, and eats the tuna by himself. We are inclined to curse the heavy man, to assert that he has committed an injustice. We are outraged that the stronger person consumes food as a relative luxury while denying the nearly dead man food as a necessity. Our egalitarian impulse that all persons have the same right to live is offended. We judge the muscular man guilty and weigh various punishments.

164

Now the rest of the story. Turn the clock backwards. The thin man is a convicted felon who raped, killed, and buried women for several years before being caught. Recently, he escaped from federal prison by stabbing a guard in the neck. His companion in the storm is a schoolteacher. Two days ago the killer walked up to the teacher's campsite and, claiming that a bear took all his food, asked for dinner. The teacher, his wife, and children gladly shared their food and wine with the stranger. The next morning the family discovered that their provisions were stolen and the stranger had disappeared. The wife spotted the escaped prisoner's photograph in a magazine, and the husband decided to pursue the killer while his family fetched the sheriff. The scales of justice are shifting right before our eyes. Now, we are sympathetic to the teacher. We judge him a hero worthy of more than a can of tuna.

The cabin scenario provides two warning flags on the road to justice. First, justice must stand upon principles and above emotions. Many outraged persons, upon witnessing the tuna scene, would strike or injure the teacher. Many crowds of decent persons have become bloodthirsty mobs in search of someone, whoever is convenient, to lynch in order to quench their thirst for revenge. Uncontrolled emotions lead to courtrooms of shouting and fist waving, not to justice. Secondly, life is more than it appears to be. Even the most perceptive persons can rarely tell at first glance the who's, where's, why's, and what's of a particular dispute. It is necessary to go back stage and study the human drama before deciding who is innocent or guilty beyond any reasonable doubt.

Justice requires continuous monitoring. Respect for

affirmen, reciprocity, and impartiality is never universal. Recently, I watched a California mayor advise church leaders to picket a movie theater that showed sexual films and to photograph, lobby, and intimidate the theater's customers. When the theater owner told police that church members were bullying his clientele, the law enforcers did nothing. The city council voted, unanimously, that it was "freedom of speech and assembly" to gather on public sidewalks outside the theater and to express one's opinions. One month later, a gas station owner informed police that Chicanos were picketing his business because of his public statements against Mexicans. The police arrested the demonstrators. The mayor and city council declared, unanimously, that this second group of sidewalk picketers were "disruptive troublemakers and trespassers." When I called attention to this contradiction at a press conference, city officials shook with anger. At such brutal times, a sense of humor and an appreciation for irony are vital.

Codified justice should be easy to understand. The best-known collection of ancient laws is the Code of Hammurabi, named after the man who ruled Babylon seventeen centuries before Christ was born. The gods, said Hammurabi, had named him to promote the welfare of the people, cause justice to prevail in the land, destroy the wicked and the evil, that the strong might not oppress the weak. His laws numbered less than three hundred and provided a pattern of order for the state and the individual. Here are two typical statues:

> 1. If a man weave a spell and bring a charge of murder against another man and has not justified himself, the accuser shall be put to death.
> 2. If a fire broke out in a man's house and a man who

has come to extinguish the fire has lifted up his eyes to the property of the householder and has taken the property of the householder, that man shall be thrown into the fire.

These laws, whatever else may be said about them, state the penalties for false accusation and theft clearly enough for every citizen to understand them. By comparison, contemporary American codes are written in obscure legalese. Our tax laws alone, not to mention other civil and criminal regulations, fill shelves in the library. Our absurdly complex system encourages the widespread belief that any criminal can escape punishment, if he can afford a sufficiently clever lawyer. Our multiplicity of laws embarrasses justice.

Only a minute fraction of human actions is governed by written law. Laws do not punish husbands who lie to wives, nor cynics who belittle everyone. Conversely, laws do not reward gardeners who beautify their yards, nor pedestrians who toss litter in trashcans. Most daily intercourse with other persons is governed by moral judgments. Moral codes prescribe conduct on three levels: morals that must be obeyed (one can not commit murder), morals that must not be disobeyed openly (one should not commit certain sex acts), and morals that counsel perfection (one should befriend all neighbors). By and large, the laws enacted by legislators focus upon the first category of morals, behavior as it affects public safety. The other two classes of behavior are enforced by peer pressure and learned conscience.

You are now at a fork in the road. A tough choice lies before you: to wit, why should you be an ethical person, rather than a villain, in matters not covered by law? There are four reasons why it is better for you and me to become an affirman. An ethical life affirms good health, success, meaning, and progress.

Integrity affirms physical and emotional well-being. Let us be blunt. Treachery creates enormous stress. Some people cannot tell the truth to save their lives. Some of these individuals are upper class tycoons, others are middle class consumers, and still more are down and out hustlers. These persons have several common characteristics, including tight jaws, nervous twitches, and high blood pressure. Their world is nightmarish. These petty Machiavellians constantly must dodge persons who can expose them, and they run frantically from their own selves. They are prime candidates for ulcers, strokes, and heart attacks. Integrity is much gentler on the body.

Malevolent persons commonly assume that everyone is as base as themselves. They absolve lying and stealing by asserting that all persons lie and steal. Their negative attitude prohibits them from befriending, respecting, or loving anyone. A vicious cycle begins. Ignominious persons become increasingly isolated from humanity. Profound loneliness sets in. This downward slide leads to depression, neurosis, and a host of crippling emotional ailments. Meanwhile, kind persons are much more likely to appreciate Charles Darwin's observation that a man's friendships are one of the best measurements of his worth. Ethical persons can reach out and touch other humans in mutually beneficial ways. As Montaigne tells us, a grief shared, halves the pain; a pleasure shared, doubles the joy.

Secondly, uprightness affirms success. Prosperous persons, save those who inherit titles and monies, apply more talent, courage, and hard work to their daily obstacles than do most persons. In most walks of life, honesty pays. It is a safe bet that, given a choice between two hardware stores, you will shop at the business that sells you wrenches only if you need them. You are unlikely to support an owner who practices the comedian W.C. Field's advice, "Never give a sucker an even break."

Evil is vastly overrated. The idea that people flourish because they are malicious is a myth. Most venomous persons are utter failures, personally and socially. Our prisons overflow with such individuals. No doubt, some of the world's prominent legislators, entertainers, advertising executives, and pillars of society are rotten to the core. But, still their treachery is a liability. Imagine two real estate investors, each of whom owns about 100 apartments. The first man, a scoundrel, is hated by his tenants and is involved in a half-dozen law suits at any given time. The second individual treats tenants respectfully and his trouble is limited to broken garbage disposals. To an affirmist, the second landlord is far more successful than the first.

Third, virtue affirms meaning. People hunger for a sense of purpose just as passionately as they need water, food, and shelter. After World War II, Helmut Thielicke delivered lectures on nihilism, extreme skepticism, at the University of Tubingen, Germany. The auditorium was packed with starving, freezing adults dressed in rags. These persons sought a reason to live after watching the annihilation of their families and towns by insane masters of war. These victims hungered for powerful, life-affirming truths to replace the impotent, life-destroying lies that Third Reich leaders had fed them. These survivors needed to reaffirm the order made possible by ethical persons after experiencing the chaos precipitated by scoundrels.

Today, many persons are just as confused as those destitute Germans in 1945. Our contemporaries' emotions are tied in knots by clever Orwellian villains: politicians, who preach that peace is a new missile system, and salesmen, who profess that rebellion is a fashionable sports car. Most of our citizens lead lives of quiet desperation because they cannot find quality beneath slick slogans. A few among us violently explode. Our people sense that the world has little liking for truthful persons and truth-seekers. We know, as did H.L. Mencken, that a Galileo could no more be elected president of the United States than he could be elected Pope of Rome. Both high posts are reserved for men favored for their ability to disguise the facts with palatable illusions. Ethics, now as always, lets us make sense of our own lives even though we are surrounded by ignorance, injustice, and senseless cruelty.

Fourth, rectitude affirms progress. People advance when they have the courage, talent, and hard work to admit their failures and to correct them. Thomas Edison remarked that he never did anything worthwhile by accident, nor did any of his inventions come by accident. He wrote, "I speak without exaggeration when I say that I have constructed three thousand different theories in connection with the electric light.... Yet, in only two cases did my experiments prove the truth of my theory." It took enormous ethical perseverance for Edison to confront 2,998 failures without throwing in the towel and lowering his goals.

It is easy to be a villain. All it takes is more ambition than talent and a willingness to take "the short cut," to cheat, in order to attain one's goals. There is enormous social and economic pressure for scientists to falsify their experimental data and to publish their fictions. Laboratory equipment is very expensive and cannot be purchased without grants, for which the competition is fierce. In addition, most administrators who allot funding are overworked and undermotivated. These judges frequently evaluate scientists by the quantity, not the quality, of articles and books that they have published. In the short term, many scientists (and researchers in all fields) profit from their lengthy bibliographies of dubious publications. Without doubt, a few persons climb and stay high in their profession by subtle fraud. But, I guarantee you, none of them will ever invent a better light bulb unless they affirm truth in the lab!

To conclude, life is a neverending war between the ethical persons and the unscrupulous in which justice favors affirmen, reciprocity, and scientific evidence. Justice and ethics prosper when persons practice the Affirmist Rule: "Affirm the best in others, as you would have others affirm the best in you."

171

IX
POWER & SUCCESS:
AN AFFIRMIST RECIPE

"I have learned that success is to be measured not so much by the position that one has achieved in life as by the obstacles which he has overcome while trying to succeed."

—Booker T. Washington

"Keep away from people who try to belittle your ambitions. Small people always do that, but the really great make you feel that you, too, can become great."

—Mark Twain

Congratulations! Power and success are not gifts for the passive many, but rewards for the active few. You, by reading this far, exclaim that you are eager to stand out, even further, from those neighbors, colleagues, and relatives who belittle your ambitions. Your actions declare that you are enthusiastic to push your talents to new frontiers. Power-seekers at every level share your passion. So let us begin an exciting journey together.

Thus far, we have explored leaders and followers, alternative immortalities, and the cries of impotence. We have demonstrated beyond any reasonable doubt that strong individuals can enrich their own lives and those of others. But a theoretical analysis of power is incomplete. Power, to be truly understood and appreciated, must be experienced. Nietzsche's WILL TO POWER and Bertrand Russell's POWER have powerful authors. Both books provide outstanding recipes that will augment your power and success if, of course, you translate their words into your actions. In this final chapter, we shall stand on the shoulders of these predecessors.

Power and success are our goals. Power is the ability to make events unfold according to a plan. Success is the capacity to earn external rewards for one's talents. Powerful individuals do not automatically receive economic or social success in return for their excellence. Bobby Fischer, who defeated Boris Spassky in 1972 for the world chess championship, endured poverty and obscurity for years because the United States did not appreciate his masterful power to defeat Kings and Queens with Pawns. Meanwhile, Spassky enjoyed relative affluence and national eminence in the Soviet Union. Conversely, successful persons do not necessarily attain power. Every town judges its "founding families" paragons of success because these persons inherit fat bank accounts, fertile lands, and famous names. Many people who inherit their success lack the initiative, intelligence, and industry to steer events on their own. Ideally, power and success are welded together.

Ten ingredients are required in order to transform the hunger for power from a vague emotion into a practical act.

First and foremost, power-seekers must believe in something greater than themselves. They must be driven by a high purpose. Many people never find a clear, longterm direction for themselves. One year these persons are romantics in search of a utopian society and, three hundred sixty-five days later, they are hardboiled cynics in pursuit of a dollar. One minute they praise the risk taking of ocean explorer Jacques Cousteau and, sixty seconds later, they commend the caution of their employer. Their opinions, feelings, and goals shift with the wind. They are like ships without rudders that drift aimlessly at sea until a captain jumps on board and steers them towards his favorite ports.

Success-seeking persons should define themselves and their ultimate purpose concisely. One sentence is ample to answer the essential questions: who are you and what do you want to achieve?

Steven Jobs exemplifies exalted purpose. Until about 1977, computers were so expensive that few persons other than employees at universities, research laboratories, and other large institutions had access to them. The average person who wanted to work with computers had to settle for primitive machines that they assembled from kits. Jobs, a 21-year-old with business acumen, and Stephen Wozniak, a 25-year-old engineer, turned this bad situation into a golden opportunity. In 1976, they designed and built Apple I, a no frills computer that was basically an electronic circuit board. When they received 50 orders, totalling $200,000, for their invention, Jobs fancied that average adults might want to purchase personal computers that were easy to use. So, the two Californians added a keyboard, memory, a disk drive, a power supply, a video terminal, and a fancy exterior to the Apple I. They called it Apple II. Their sales jumped to $7,000,000 in the next year. By 1979, Wozniak effectively retired from Apple to go back to school and to sponsor music festivals. By 1980, sales skyrocketed to $117,000,000. An entire industry was born with Jobs at the helm.

Jobs, the adopted son of a machinist, catapulted a tiny business founded in a Los Gatos, California garage into one of America's five hundred largest corporations in the incredibly short period of only five years. Apple's meteoric rise enabled him, at age 29, to become one of America's one hundred richest persons. The youngest of the hundred, he is one of only seven persons on that elite list who earned, rather than inherited, their fortunes.

Clearly, Apple's cofounder is both powerful and successful. But back to the point at hand. Jobs is intelligent enough to realize that fame and fortune do not insure fulfillment. During the turbulent 1960's and the Vietnam War, he liked Bob Dylan's protest music and Eastern mysticism. While a student at Reed College in Oregon, Jobs was influenced by poet Gary Snyder and by counter-culture leader and drug experimenter Timothy Leary. Jobs fueled the idealism of the sixties with personal discipline. The result was his desire to improve not only his own condition, but to mold a better world. Jobs stated this high purpose when he tried to persuade John Sculley, the president of Pepsi-Cola soft drink company, to become Apple's chief administrator. Jobs asked the reluctant Sculley, "Are you going to keep selling sugar water to children when you could be changing the world?"

A dynamic purpose is essential but, like any ideal, it is only a start. Earth is overcrowded with wishful, high-minded persons who promise us inventions, revolutions, and masterpieces that never materialize. These dreamers remind the power-seeker that talk is cheap, while labor is dear. Ideals must be subordinated into useful goals before power is possible. These goals must be specific, measurable, and realistic. These goals must refer to a definite period of time.

Useful goals are specific. Many scientists, entrepreneurs, and social commentators believe that the computer is the most flexible tool yet invented by man. They appreciate that computers serve as printing presses, communication centers, filing systems, number crunchers, and artistic instruments. These futurists have a goal. They dream of a 20th century information revolution which will provide intellectual energy inexpensively the way the 19th century petrochemical revolution supplied mechanical energy cheaply. So far so good. But their goal is abstract. It is too vague. Jobs stands out from the crowd because his goal is specific. He is leading efforts to manufacture and market low cost computers to homes and schools, so that children can learn how to program computers as naturally as they discover how to read, write, and count. These empowered children will lead society from the Industrial Age to the Information Age.

Useful goals are measurable. They provide standards by which people evaluate their success and failure. Sometimes, goals can be expressed numerically. A fullback may declare that his season will be good, if he carries the football 200 times for a total of 800 yards, if his team wins 11 games and loses 5, and if he plays all sixteen games without an injury. On other occassions, goals may be measured more subjectively. Suppose an artist aspires to paint bathing girls as well as Renoir. Once her painting is finished, she must devise a method for comparing it with Renoir's work. She may, for example, ask art critics whom she respects to vote on whether her, or Renoir's, painting is better (without, of course, telling her judges who painted which canvas). Or she may invent her own criteria for deciding whose brushstrokes and colors are superior. In either case, she needs a method for measuring her progress just as much as the football player or any other power-seeker.

Useful goals are realistic. They correspond with a person's talents and resources. William Faulkner, one of this century's premier novelists, said that the only tools he needed for his writing were paper, tobacco, food, and a little whiskey. Well, what worked for the Oxford, Mississippi author is not so relevant to everyone. Thousands of persons who fantasize about writing the great American novel expend more energy lifting whiskey glasses than putting words onto paper. Their idle dreams are ultimately a waste of time. The power-seeker understands himself well enough to pick goals that are not too high and not too low. He tries, first, to write an adequate novel. If he succeeds at that, he reevaluates himself and sharpens his craft until he eventually writes a good novel. It is by building and climbing solid steps, not by flights of fancy, that real power is attained.

Useful goals refer to a definite time period. This fact is put into practice by all powerful institutions. The United States' House of Representatives, the General Motors Board of Directors, and the University of California's Regents project future income, expenses, and policies as accurately as they can. The leaders of these organizations realize that success depends upon detailed short-term and long-term planning. The power-seeker approaches life with a similar rationality. When persons tell him that it is cold and machine-like to make his future happen according to a plan, he realizes that he is listening to followers who submit to institutions because they cannot emulate them. Each person should plan goals for that day, that month, that year, and the next five years. Napoleon spelled out the importance of advance preparation:

> If I seem equal to the occassion, and ready to face it when it comes, it is because I have thought the matter over a long time before undertaking it.... I have antici-

pated whatever might happen. It is no genie which suddenly reveals to me what I ought to do or say, ... but my own reflection.

Courage is the second ingredient for power. Every person, no matter how comfortable his life may appear to an outsider, has hardships. Philosopher David Hume, in a moment of despair, remarked that most people are born into anguish, reared with impotence and despair, and end in agony and horror. We disagree with the Scottish historian's gloom. Nonetheless, life is saturated with dreadful events. We can become diseased, our homes can burn, and our neighbors can declare war upon us. A coward flees backward, away from these perils. A courageous person steps forward, into life's challenges.

Persons manifest courage in numerous ways. Artists, coal miners, and football players confront the occupational hazards of public ridicule, cave-ins, and dislocated shoulders, respectively. When successful, these persons acquire an appropriate valor. They learn to confront danger without giving in to fear. Usually, persons exhibit courage in one situation and cowardice in another. A karate master may fearlessly assess and subdue villains who bully the rest of us, but may be afraid to admit that his brother is a thief. We herald bravery in its multiforms. And we recognize that the most powerful, successful persons become courageous towards life in general, not just within the confines of a job or hobby. Let us examine the two most common forms of courage, ethical and physical, with case studies.

Rachel Carson personifies ethical courage. To find out how, we must step back into history. Humankind has carried out an age-old war against mosquitos, ants, and other insects. In 1874, a German chemist named Othmar

179

Zeidler synthesized a new chemical called dichloro-diphenyl-trichlorethane that would make a profound impact on our Earth. Paul Muller, a research chemist at the J.R. Geigy Company in Switzerland, discovered in 1939 that man-made DDT was extraordinarily effective at killing insects. After a series of tests against the Colorado potato beetle, the boll weevil, and lice, DDT's potency was confirmed, and Muller won the Nobel Prize for his discovery.

DDT was considered a miracle. It was highly lethal to insects, almost insoluble in water, and relatively not toxic to mammals and humans. Many chemical companies, farmers, food processors, and grocery chains were euphoric. At last the war had been won! This enthusiasm was picked up by the general public. By the 1950s and 60s, many citizens used lawnmover attachments and pumps to spray DDT in their yards. With religious and military zeal, many communities even boasted about the number of tons of DDT sprayed over their cities by airplanes each year. These persons believed that man's purpose was to control nature, even if they did not understand it.

But DDT, like all miracles, fell short of expectations. As early as 1945, Charles Cottam and Elmer Higgins of the U.S. Fish and Wildlife Service issued warnings against using DDT as an insecticide. By the 1960's, reports from around the world signaled that a serious danger was in the air. DDT was found in the fatty tissues of Eskimos, in the soils of Canadian forests, and in bodies of Antarctica's penguins. These areas were far away from spraying regions, which indicated that DDT was being transported high in our atmosphere and being deposited in precipitation around the globe. Something was wrong in man's dream of an insect-free Garden of Eden.

Carson entered this drama well-prepared. Born in 1907 on a small farm, she spent much of her childhood walking alone in fields and woods. This love of the outdoors sparked Rachel to become a life long bird watcher. Her rural background also prompted her to focus on zoology at the Pennsylvania College for Women and to earn her M.A. in genetics at Johns Hopkins. For years, she labored as a relatively anonymous government employee in Washington, D.C. while writing magazine articles and books on the side. All this changed with her publication of a best-selling trilogy about the sea: THE SEA AROUND US, UNDER THE SEA-WIND, and THE EDGE OF THE SEA. These books earned her an enthusiastic audience.

By the late 1950s, scientist and naturalist Carson became interested in the slow but steady disappearance of many birds. Populations of carnivorous birds were particularly hurt. The peregrine falcon, whose fast flights and dramatic dives after prey have made it legendary, was common in New England in the 1940s but was vanishing. The osprey, commonly called the "Fish Eagle" because it feeds entirely on fish, no longer returned to its yearly nests along the East Coast. Even the white pelican, which was once so abundant along the Florida and Gulf coasts that they seemed to be everywhere, were gone from their seashore pilings. What was happening to these birds? Nobody knew. The baffling mystery awaited a courageous investigator.

Carson was the detective called into action. One of her correspondents asked her to help prohibit the government from spraying a private bird reserve near Cape Cod, Massachusetts. Carson asked questions about the spraying and was alarmed by what she learned. So she set out to study the effects of spraying on plants and animals.

Soon, a Long Island group opposed to the spraying of gypsy moths asked her to testify at a trial. One step led to another and, reluctantly, Carson started writing a book about what was killing the birds and why humans might be the next victims. She hesitated for good reasons. Carson was seriously ill with cancer. In addition, she had arthritis, she had a mother in poor health, and she had an adopted young boy to take care for.

These misfortunes did not stop heroine Carson. In 1962, she published SILENT SPRING. Her book documented brutally and accurately the effects of DDT. She explained how plants absorb and accumulate DDT from the water, soil, and atmosphere; how herbivores take in DDT from plants; and how carnivores gather DDT from their food. Her analysis of the food chain demonstrated that when we poison mosquitos with massive doses of DDT (or other toxins) we are indirectly poisoning ourselves. Carson's lucid style introduced the concept of ecology to the general public and made her the founder of the environmental movement.

SILENT SPRING was viciously attacked by critics. A lawyer for one of the chemical firms threatened to sue Carson's publisher and suggested that she was a Communist. The attorney reasoned that Carson wanted to destroy American agriculture, to reduce our production to that of Iron Curtain countries. Others condemned her for preferring birds to persons. Physicians, corporate presidents, and agriculture consultants lambasted her as a fanatic defender of nature. Still others cursed her for not being a medical doctor, or for not being a wife and mother. TIME, a popular magazine of our era, wrote, "Many scientists sympathize with Miss Carson's love of wildlife.... But they fear that her emotional and inaccurate outburst in

SILENT SPRING may do harm by alarming the nontechnical public, while doing no good for the things that she loves.''

Carson remained silent during these attacks against her successful campaign to save your health and mine. She was dying. She did not live to witness the banning of DDT or the flourishing of her environmental movement. The modest birdwatcher returned to the soil before she could read TIME's new section, "The Environment," which accompanied a photograph of her. Rachel Carson believed that biological life is more valuable than corporate profits, and she remained resolute in her just cause. For this reason, she became one of her generation's most influential persons. Carson prevailed.

Courage requires effective action. It is inadequate to be brave in the safety of one's private fantasies. Carson was courageous not primarily because she wrote SILENT SPRING, but because she made her book available for public debate. She was courageous not simply because she wrote against DDT (and other toxic substances), but because she gathered persuasive evidence to argue her position. Carson's power to alter the United States' agricultural policy testifies that she grasped how, where, and when to deliver her message for maximum impact. On the road to victory, all venturesome persons practice Spinoza's advice that flight at the proper time, just as well as fighting, is to be reckoned as showing strength of mind.

Physical courage takes us directly to Louis Pasteur. In the early 19th century, people suffered from many illnesses that no longer haunt us. Anthrax is a disease that often attacked cattle, sheep, and horses. Humans commonly contracted it by touching animal hairs or hides. Today, anthrax is treated with penicllin or tetracyolines.

Rabies is an infectious disease of mammals, mainly carnivores. Humans often caught this ailment, which led to paralysis and death, through the bite of rabid dogs. In our time, rabies is controlled with both a vaccination and a serum.

Pasteur, a French chemist and biologist, was not as lucky as we. His best and brightest contemporaries had little idea what caused diseases. They did not understand the connection between Bacillus anthracis and anthrax or between a neurotropic filtrable virus present in the saliva of rabid animals and rabies. In 1798, twenty-four years before Pasteur's birth, Edward Jenner had discovered a vaccination for smallpox. But nobody could apply Jenner's breakthrough to the many other infections that plagued humanity. Medicine was at a standstill and in need of a visionary.

The tool for better vision already existed. Almost two hundred years before Pasteur, Antony Van Leeuwenhoek combined small glass lenses with very short focal length into a compound microscope. His instruments, some of which could magnify objects an amazing 300 times, allowed Leeuwenhoek to glimpse into the previously unseen and unimagined world of microbes. The extremely patient observer learned that even a drop of ordinary water teemed with life, with what he called "little animalcules." Turning his attention to humans, the Dutch inventor was the first person to describe spermatozoa and one of the first to give an account of red blood corpuscles. He studied human mouths and intestines. There, no doubt to his surprise, he found a rich interplay of bacteria and protozoa.

Medicine had not yet applied Leeuwenhoek's findings to human health. A few researchers such as

Fracastoro and Henle had proposed that microbes might cause diseases, but they offered little proof. Enter Pasteur. Fermentation is the oxidative decomposition of complex substances due to bacteria, molds, yeasts, and other microorganisms. This process helps produce alcohol and bake bread. By studying fermentation, Pasteur verified that certain microorganisms can cause undesirable byproducts. This led him to imagine that microorganisms can also harm cattle, humans, and other animals.

Imagine the dangers confronting Pasteur. In order for him to test the hypothesis that germs caused diseases, he had to examine microorganisms in his laboratory that may well have killed him upon contact. This was long before antiseptic measures, such as spraying equipment with carbolic acid, were known. And, even if he could insulate himself from harmful germs, he had no reliable way of distinguishing between safe and lethal microbes. For years, Pasteur risked life and limb peering into bottles of toxic materials. To say the least, the courageous scientist's efforts paid off. Pasteur invented a process to kill microorganisms in liquids such as milk ("pasteurization"), a method to immunize cattle against anthrax, a technique to innoculate people against rabies, and a vaccine to prevent chicken cholera. His basic principles have been extended by others to protect humans against still other diseases.

Pasteur was courageous because his calculated behavior was neither foolhearty nor fearful. He understood the risks that he took and avoided unnecessary ones. A person who attempts to cure diseases without knowledge of biology and physiology is no hero. Wandering from one hospital patient to another, he will likely die in short order from contagious infections, killing many innocent persons

185

in route. Such a person is a fool, whose efforts are based on ignorance. An individual, for example a physician, who tries to save patients without summoning a second opinion is no hero. Such a person is a coward, who fears that his reputation will be tarnished if he admits to less than perfection.

Work is the third ingredient for power. This statement may sound trivial, but it is not. Countless persons have a superstitious attitude about power. These weak individuals would have us believe that the only difference between themselves and Thomas Watson, Sr. is that he was "lucky." Watson, according to their delusion, simply knew the right persons, had a proper smile, and owned a charm bracelet. They are terribly naive. Watson transformed small factories that manufactured grocery store scales and time clocks into IBM, what is now the world's largest computer company, by laboring. He worked a 112 hour week for years and never took a vacation.

Power-seekers face two decisions regarding work. First, they must decide what kind of work to do. Most people work in order to live. Unless they strike oil in their backyard, please their rich parents, or collect government welfare checks, they must labor in return for the money required to pay their bills. Individuals react quite differently to this fact of life. Some decide to work grudgingly, others gratefully. Some select to work as humans, others as machines. No work is so boring that someone cannot enliven it; no work so crude that someone cannot exalt it; and no work so impassive that someone cannot humanize it. Weak persons work grudgingly and as machines. Powerful persons select professions, occupations, and hobbies that they can enliven, exalt, and humanize.

Work, as philosopher Paul Kurtz noted in EXUBER-ANCE, is the fullest expression of human power. We are not saying that any chore chosen at random empowers and satifies everyone. Professional weight lifters find more exuberance in moving furniture than do tax accountants. Work fulfills persons only when it leads them closer to their high purposes. Earl Warren, Chief Justice of the United States Supreme Court, reread legal documents that would bore most people to death because mastering, the law was his purpose. The vast majority of persons labor in behalf of their boss's goals, not their own. Powerful persons are those who find a way to escape this deadend.

Secondly, powerful persons must decide how much time to devote towards their high purpose. There is ample time for you to succeed. Average Americans work a forty hour week. Assuming they sleep eight hour nights, only 36% of their waking moments are committed to earning a living. This fact opens the door for your future. Even if you are burdened with full-time obligations that are opposed to your talents, 64% of your time remains to bring about your dreams. "Come on," you ask, "Who has the energy to finish eight hours of drudgery and start new projects?" The answer is simple: powerful persons.

Successful persons work overtime for themselves. Barbara Tuchman wanted to write history books. However, she was a mother and a wife who did not belong to the academic world. She made the time to overcome both obstacles. Between washing dishes and vacuuming rugs, she took five years to author her first book, BIBLE AND SWORD. She spent another seven years to complete A DISTANT MIRROR: THE CALAMITOUS 14th CEN-TURY. Tuchman put her heart and mind into these works. They were labors of love. As a result, she has a larger audience than any other serious historian in our time. Tuchman was awarded two Pulitzer Prizes and named president of the American Academy of Arts and Letters (the first woman to hold this position). Another mother and housewife was Betty Friedan. When she told persons that she wanted to write a book about women, they thought she was crazy. Well, Friedan got a baby-sitter three days a week and took a bus to the New York Public Library. The rest is history. Her book, THE FEMININE MYSTIQUE, earned her national and, then, worldwide celebrity. Alvin Toffler, author of FUTURE SHOCK, asserted, "Betty Friedan is to the worldwide sex-role revolution what Tom Paine was to the American Revolution." Think for a moment. On the average, all persons have about the same amount of time. Time, the distance between birth and death, is the great equalizer.

Many persons have a forty-hour a week headstart on housewifes Tuchman and Friedan. They own businesses, direct symphony orchestras, teach university students, or otherwise earn incomes doing what they enjoy. But few entrepreneurs, musicians, and professors can excel by working only a forty-hour week. All other variables being equal, they will accomplish twice as much in eighty hours. These extra hours reduce candlelight dinners with spouses, poker games with friends, and picnics with the kids. Not everybody is happy with these tradeoffs. So, power-seekers must make tough choices about how their social life and work life will interrelate.

Let us say the unpopular. Powerful persons live in order to work. They agree with Thomas Carlyle, "Blessed is the man that has found his work." And they realize that nothing is really work unless you would rather be doing something else. Weak persons condemn "workaholics" as sick, because these powerless persons have never found any activity that they truly love. One of life's pleasures is to concentrate so intensely on a stock report, a chessboard, or a puzzle that four hours go by as if a minute. One of life's thrills is to run a twenty-six mile marathon, invent a medicine, or unearth a Mayan ruin.

Power-seekers should embrace creative, productive work with zest. Do not work, as do Puritans, to prove yourselves worthy of Providence. Do not labor, as do sterile bureaucrats, to flee human interaction. Do not toil, as do Freud's stereotypes, to repress eroticism. Toss aside these negatives. Push yourselves because all growth depends upon activity. All physical, social, and intellectual progress depends upon exertion. Work is not a curse, but rather the prerogative of intelligent persons who want more out of life than hollow dreams. And, when you feel tired, remember Pablo Picasso. The French painter created an average of five paintings a week for seventy-five years! Most of his work was done standing, often in cold rooms. You and he have the same amount of time in a day.

Perseverance is the fourth ingredient of power. Society has more than enough educated and talented persons who never succeed. And it is almost a truism that genius is ignored. Power-seekers, whatever their education and talent may be, must continue steadfastly in the face of constant discouragement. Step into the shoes of one of America's most eminent "losers." In 1831, he was defeated in business. In 1832, he was defeated in an election for the legislature. In 1834, he was defeated in his bid to become Speaker of the legislature. In 1843, he was he defeated in an election for Congress. In 1855, he was defeated in an election for the Senate. Finally, in 1860, he was elected President of the United States. This famous failure was Abraham Lincoln.

Lincoln achieved success because he stood up and walked away from a series of painful setbacks. His childhood, with all its hardships, had given Lincoln the will to persevere. Winston Churchill, the British Prime Minister during World War II, also realized that the world moves aside for persons who boldly push forward. Britain was threatened by Nazi Germany's far superior military. But Churchill would not surrender. He convinced his countrymen that they would not fail or falter, that no sudden battle shock or long-drawn trial would wear them down. His perpetual pushing and reassuring gave Great Britain the confidence it needed to outlive Hitler's death machine.

Life can resemble the fable about the tortoise and the hare. Once upon a time, there was a race between a swift rabbit with long hindlegs and a slow turtle with short legs. The rabbit took victory for granted and, everytime it got ahead in the race, played around and waited for the turtle to catch up. The hare then sprinted ahead and laughed at its slow competitor. In the end, the turtle won.

Many intelligent, resourceful persons glow brightly in their youth and grow dim as adults. Flip through your dusty, old school yearbooks. No doubt, some of those voted "most likely to succeed" by your classmates have, or will, become miserable alcoholics by the age of forty. Other less highly regarded youths have, or will, become mayors, corporate presidents, scientists, and other leaders. These role reversals happen every day. Some persons slowly and methodically climb over the financial, social, sexual, and professional hurdles that make up the obstacle course of adulthood. When they fall on their face, they get up and start over again. Often, nobody recognizes these persons until they have surpassed everyone else.

Powerful persons are, by definition, exceptions to the rule. They prevail whether they began life with a bang or a whimper. Raymond Kurzweil was a fast starter. He says that, at age five, he knew he would become a famous, successful scientist. He is now younger than forty and is a technological genius. One of his inventions enables blind people to read, and he will soon unveil a talking telephone for deaf people. By contrast, Muhammad was a slow starter. He was born into poverty in Mecca, at that time an insignificant town. He remained illiterate, according to Islamic tradition, and showed no promise of being an exceptional person until after the age of forty. Within his latter years, he became one of the world's major religious and military leaders.

Ronald Gross, a foremost spokesman for independent thinkers, calls our attention to a third case. Buckminister Fuller was both exceedingly fast and painfully slow. On the fast side, he was often decades ahead of his time. "If I aim to be fifty years ahead of my time I shall be safe. No one will interfere with me because I'll be so far ahead that I will pose no threat to all the people who have a vested interest in opposing progress. They'll just call me a nut," he said. In 1938, he was one of the first persons who wrote about practical applications of Einstein's theory of relativity. Surely enough, a prospective publishing house rejected his manuscript as "charlatanry." (Einstein, after reading Fuller's manuscript, was impressed and commended it to a publisher!). Fuller went on to invent geodesic domes, which are still way ahead of today's architecture; the Dymaxion automobile, which outperformed cars built fifty years afterwards; and the Dymaxion map, which first represented the Earth's continents without distortion. In 1972, a businessman told Fuller of a new industry, the mass production of bathrooms. Well, Fuller had designed the first one forty-five years before.

On the slow side, Fuller had a difficult time earning a living. Fuller and his father-in-law founded Stockade Building Company in Chicago in order to produce a new kind of building system they had developed. Outsiders took over the company and, in 1927, fired Fuller without severance pay. It wasn't his first, or last, economic failure. But, this time, the not yet immortal "Bucky" hit rock bottom. "I've done the best I know how and it hasn't worked. I guess I'm just no good; people seem to think so; even my mother has always been afraid that I was worthless. I guess she was right," he said to himself. Leaving his wife and young child in their apartment, he walked towards Lake Michigan's shore. He fully expected to end his life.

Fuller stopped short of suicide. For, in his despair, he realized that he did not have the right to kill himself. He saw that he, and all humans, are here for each other. The inventor from Chicago persevered in spite of the darkness that engulfed him. All powerful persons, whether they are child prodigies or adult plodders, share this will to prevail.

The ability to rise above popularity is the fifth ingredient of power. Young, ambitious persons everywhere imagine fame as the end of the rainbow. They long to hear crowds roar approval for their actions and crave to read journalists praise their virtues. Their fantasies are natural and healthy. Life can be terribly cold and indifferent to their fates. To be desired by other persons warms their lives. However, striving persons should realize that the vast majority of powerful persons are not applauded for

192

their talents, labors, or sacrifices.

Lack of acclaim has three origins. First and foremost, potent persons' contributions are usually beyond the public's grasp. The list of immortals who suffered from anonymity in their lifetimes is sobering. Vincent Van Gogh, whose paintings are now more precious than gold, could not find anyone to purchase his works. Subsequently, he committed suicide. Gregor Mendel, whose principles of heredity are now foundations of biology, was ignored by his era's scientists. He died a lonely monk. Some persons are more fortunate. Frank Wilczek is one of today's eminent physicists whose equations help explain invisible, subatomic particles called quarks. Wilczek's work is understood and respected by a couple thousand scientists. Even so, many humans weaker than he are applauded by far larger crowds.

Secondly, powerful persons are rarely hailed because of general apathy. Most persons simply do not care who supplies them with energy, technology, and culture. As long as society appears to function smoothly, the masses take the most productive citizens for granted in every region of the Earth. Ordinary citizens, by and large, do not want to know who controls their lives. These followers resent being told how television producers, newspaper publishers, and business tycoons manipulate their values, because this obvious truth makes them feel like pawns under the hand of kings and queens. The great chessboard of life is too real for them to confront. So, they are not about to exert themselves praising their masters.

The third origin is the most ironic. Namely, powerful persons are most fully understood by their competitors. We have already discussed Stephen Jobs of Apple Computer and Thomas Watson, Sr. of rival International

Business Machines. These entrepreneurs, as do the President of the United States and the Premier of the Soviet Union, share much more with each other than they do with their subordinates. However, it is rare for opponents to honor each other publicly. They tend to keep their mutual admiration secret.

Popularity is hard to resist. Most children learn to enjoy being patted on the back. They intuit that, if their opinions and actions are contrary to the norm, this social approval will cease. Logically enough, they flatter their teachers and emulate their peers at every opportunity. Little changes in later life. As adults, these same persons learn that popular employees get the easiest job assignments and the quickest raises. Sensibly enough, they eat lunch with and flatter their bosses whenever possible.

Power-seekers should not waste energy seeking popularity. Popular opinion, as Thomas Carlyle noted, is the greatest lie in the world. For centuries, the world's authorities and followers believed the Earth was flat. And, today, equally grand delusions are held sacred. Powerful persons satisfy their own consciences and do not trouble themselves looking for fame. They already have a high purpose, which is its own reward. To seek fame as an end, persons must direct their lives so as to please the fancy of others, not themselves. This pursuit lends itself more readily to mediocrity than to power.

People are notoriously fickle. Entertainers, clothiers, novelists, and all persons who deal with the public either face this fact or sink. One month Beethoven, ruffled dresses, and Gothic romances are fashionable. The next month Rock Stars, leather skirts, and spy thrillers are the talk of the town. Henry Fielding, the 18th century English novelist, wrote that fashion is the great governor of the world. It presides not only in manners of dress and amusement, but in law, politics, religion, and all other things of the gravest kind. Particular acts have been universally received in some epochs and, at other times, universally rejected.

Sometimes, fads are silly. We are inclined to treat these fashions humorlessly, as uglinesses so intolerable that we have to alter them every month. But the pendulum that swings between social orthodoxies is not always funny. Changes in public taste can be dangerous. Nowhere is this hazard clearer than in the tragic case of J. Robert Oppenheimer.

Oppenheimer was one of our century's most brilliant persons. Born the son of a wealthy textile importer, he began his formal studies at New York's Ethical Culture School. There he studied Greek, Latin, French, and German, as well as all the available science and mathematics courses. His record earned him a place at Harvard University, where he focused on physics and graduated at the top of his class, summa cum laude. Two years later, at the age of twenty-three, he earned his Ph.D. in Germany after working with the immortal physicist, Max Born. Clearly, he was bright. In later years, he learned enough Italian in one month to read Dante, sufficient Dutch in six weeks to deliver a lecture, and the proper Sanskrit in a year to read the BHAGAVAD-GITA. But Oppenheimer's mental quickness is just the beginning of his remarkable journey.

Hitler was at large. By 1940 his march to subdue the Earth's "inferior races" was in high gear. His army had subdued Denmark, Norway, Belgium, France and the Netherlands. In September 1940, Germany met with Italy and Japan to decide how the world would be divided amongst them. This Tripartite Pact declared that Italy would rule the Mediterranean, Japan southeast Asia, and Germany central Africa. But this was not nearly enough territory for the insatiable Hitler. On June 22, 1941, he double-crossed Stalin and plunged 145 Nazi divisions into Soviet territory. His instructions to the Wehrmacht, his army, were straightforward: first, kill every Communist, intellectual, and captured enemy soldier and, secondly, bring back ordinary citizens for slave labor in Germany.

Oppenheimer was deeply disturbed by maniac Hitler's triumphs. In addition, the physicist was told that Third Reich scientists were developing a secret weapon that would bring the world to its knees. These circumstances persuaded Oppenheimer to accept an assignment that, if successful, would alter history. He agreed to head a Los Alamos, New Mexico laboratory and to direct the Manhattan Project. His job was to design, construct, and test the first atomic bomb.

The theoretical scientist surprised everyone. Not only was he an adept thinker, but he became an outstanding leader of men and women. Beginning in 1942, he persuaded one hundred American colleagues to leave their cozy research centers and homes behind and to follow him to a secret military base in the middle of nowhere. He accomplished this first step without being able to inform them what their mission would be. Within three years, he headed a small town of three thousand persons, whom he inspired to work at a feverish pace.

In July 1945, Oppenheimer looked across the New Mexico sands and watched the first atomic fireball expand in the sky. His reaction was ambivalent. He was both proud of his personal accomplishment and saddened by the explosion before his eyes. Later, he would say that his first conscious thought was, "I am become death, the shatterer of worlds." A month later, two atomic bombs were dropped, one on Hiroshima, the second on Nagaski, killing 75,000 and 39,000 persons respectively.

Oppenheimer's success made him godlike to many persons. Lewis Strauss, a trustee of the prestigious Institute for Advanced Study at Princeton, virtually begged "Oppie" to direct the institute. Oppie accepted. Under Secretary of State Dean Acheson, later to become chief architect of the Cold War, asked the hero for physics lessons. Oppie accepted. President Harry Truman asked him, in 1946, when the Russians would develop an atomic bomb. The six-foot, 120 pound celebrity said he did not know. To which Truman responded, "Never." By this, the President meant that Oppie's supernatural powers could never be duplicated. Everyone chose the dark-haired riddle to represent America's scientific community at the United Nations Conference on International Control of Atomic Energy. Oppie accepted. Wherever he turned, J.Robert Oppenheimer could do no wrong.

Beware, power-seekers, of being worshipped! Excessive adoration is a deceptive calm before an inevitable storm. Those who judge you divine because your powers far exceed theirs are gullible. And, when gullible persons discover that you are not perfect, they will declare you diabolical. Oppie's admirers were pushing him into a dangerous corner. As chief advisor on atomic policy, he intuited this trap. He complained that his proposals were being uncritically accepted. Unfortunately, Oppie did not know how to undeify himself.

In September 1949, the Soviet Union exploded its first nuclear devise. Panic swept through America. Ordinary citizens and government officials could not believe that

Russia, too, had a god on her side. Oppie's gullible flock assumed that spies must be at work. In short order, they executed Julius and Ethel Rosenberg for passing secrets to the Russians. On another front, Edward Teller proposed that the United States develop an even more "Super" weapon, the hydrogen bomb. Oppie reacted coolly to Teller's suggestion and, thereby, set the fickle public against himself.

It was not long before Lewis Strauss and others went on the offense. They accused Oppenheimer of being a threat to the United States for not enthusiastically supporting the H-bomb. They sought to strip him of his security clearance. Towards this end, Oppie was tried before a three-member panel called the Personnel Security Board. All three judges were hand picked by Strauss, once Oppie's enthusiastic supporter. Three weeks and 990 transcript pages later, the trial was over. The Federal Bureau of Investigation had more material for its four foot six inch thick file on Oppie. The physicist was found guilty of giving his masters bad advice. Soon afterwards, the Atomic Energy Commission ruled Oppenheimer unfit for future service.

J. Robert Oppenheimer was ruined. He retained his title as Director, Institute for Advanced Study (Strauss recommended that to the trustees!), but Oppie's eyes filled with sadness. Virtually nobody defended him at the end. All those admiring colleagues, who secretly resented his brilliance, had their revenge at last. They could watch the destruction of a man greater than themselves. Oppie played a dual role. He was history's master and victim. The masses gave him fame when he reflected their virtues, infamy when he mirrored their flaws. In 1967, Oppie died silently of throat cancer.

The wisdom to remain silent is the sixth ingredient of power. This lesson is often unpalatable. The vast majority of persons are talkers, not listeners. They would never hear you, if they were not waiting for their cue to speak next. A sizeable minority of humans are monologists, not hearkeners. Their tongues rotate so endlessly that they must die before echoes can catch their last words! Silence empowers persons in three ways. First, the absence of sound enables individuals to focus and sharpen their mental energy. Try to solve a crossword puzzle, balance a checkbook, or read a suspenseful novel while your neighbor is cutting oak trees with a chainsaw. Noise disrupts concentration just as surely as cold wind tightens muscles. Successful persons fully realize this advantage of silence. Accordingly, they reside in the most private, quiet locations that they can afford. By contrast, many persons are perfectly comfortable in crowded apartment buildings where televisions, stereos, and loud talkers compete for dominance. Silence makes these unfocused persons nervous, because they do not like their own company.

Secondly, silence helps persons comprehend the world. One of my favorite cartoons shows a man standing on a New York street corner surrounded by a sea of richly diverse people. The caption reads: "Kepler's fourth law says you are not the center of the universe." Excessive talkers dispute this fourth law. They do not bother to look at, listen to, or empathize with you because they already know everything (just ask them). Quite to the contrary, power-seekers learn to look and listen. Buckminister Fuller reportedly quit talking for two years, while he figured out what to do with his life. And, then, there is the provocative legend about Einstein. His parents feared that he was retarded because he did not babble like other little kids. One evening at the dinner table, Einstein startled his parents by speaking in complete sentences. When they asked him why he had been quiet so long, the genius answered, "I didn't have anything to say."

Selective listening strengthens us. Andre Kostelantz, a orchestra conductor, observed that most persons listen too much to the telephone and too little to nature. For the American musician, the wind was a favorite sound. A lonely sound, but soothing. He reminded us that power-seekers should have personal sounds that they listen for, sounds that exhilarate and enliven them, sounds that quiet and calm them. These special sounds are the heartbeat of power. You must find them before you can become your own drummer.

Thirdly, silence can aid survival. This truth is explicit in wartime. Franklin Delano Roosevelt was convinced that Hitler would crush Britain unless the United States entered World War II. The President, also, realized that Americans were opposed (before Pearl Harbor) to enter the war. Therefore, in order to save Britain, Roosevelt remained silent about the secret support that he channeled to her. Back in Europe, Winston Churchill had advance knowledge that Germans were going to massacre a town. He could have saved the town but remained silent, so that the Third Reich would not discover that its secret codes were being intercepted and decoded. Roosevelt and Churchill understood that agonizing silence at the right time can save many lives in the longterm.

Discretion is equally essential in peacetime. There are many shining human qualities, but few are as useful as knowing when, where, how, and with whom to speak. Without sound judgment, learning is pedantry; wit is insolence; and virtue is weakness. Power-seekers confront situations constantly that test their patience.

Consider one common irritant, the excruciatingly boring committee meeting. Many people serve on committees in order to add titles to their resumes, not in order to formulate effective policies. It is tempting to grab these people by the collar and declare, "Look, you've got your title. So quit coming to meetings. The rest of us have work to do." But, if you speak this candidly, you will invite a lifelong enemy and accomplish little. You will be more successful by drawing up short agendas and selecting no nonsense members. Better still, power comes to those who circumvent all unproductive meetings.

Respect for reality is the seventh ingredient of power. Reality has never been as popular as mythology, superstition, and delusion. Most people believe that a pleasant illusion is better than a harsh reality. In order to maintain their illusion, they practice self-deception. Cigarette addicts convince themselves that their lungs are exempt from cancer because they have thick blood; parents persuade themselves that their hoodlum children are misunderstood angels; and elected officials satisfy themselves that their votes are not influenced by campaign contributions. These weak individuals, more often than not, would rather die than abandon their illusions.

Most people believe what they want to believe. They do not examine the world with open eyes and minds. Rather, they select data that makes them feel good and ignore the rest. A foremost magician and debunker of nonsense, James "Amazing" Randi, gives an excellent example in his book, FLIM-FLAM! In 1978, a Canadian radio program asked the New Jersey author to participate in a telephone interview. Randi agreed and suggested a novel idea for the show. He instructed the host to tell his audience that an astro-graphologist would be available next week and that listeners should mail their birthdates and handwriting samples to the radio station. The following week, Randi was on the air. He was identified by a fictitious name, a nom de charlatan.

Randi posed as an expert astrologer and handwriting analyst. His self-appointed task was to tell three listeners, who were on the air via telephone, about themselves based on his reading of the materials that they sent to the station. In return, the three callers rated Randi's insights on a scale from one to ten. "One" meant that Randi was totally inaccurate about them; "ten" signified that he was right on target. Randi was very successful and, no doubt, stunned the audience. On the first ballot, he earned scores of nine, ten, and ten. His grade card was changed to a perfect three tens after the first guest reevaluated Randi's remarks. Randi stated that this fellow disliked hard work, but the listener insisted that he was a laborer and thus accustomed to hard work. "But" Randi countered, "I said that you disliked hard work." "True," he replied. "I guess you're right. I don't really like it."

This episode ended with a strange twist. In reality, Randi had neither birthdates nor penmanship specimens for the three listeners. He read, word for word, three analyses that had been given months before in Las Vegas for three members of a television audience! When it was revealed that Randi was a hoaxer, and his real name was announced, the three previously impressed listeners hung up their telephones. They believed Randi's deception because they wanted to believe in an authority figure who took the time to talk about them. Like scared persons everywhere, the three adults were willing to distort the facts of their own lives in order to fit into someone else's fiction (astro-graphology). They hung up because they could not face how easily they had been deluded.

Power-seekers create agreeable realities at the expense of fanciful illusions. In the late 1930s, Alfred Kinsey was asked to coordinate Indiana University's interdisciplinary course on marriage. To his surprise, he was unable to find a formal statistical study on an activity as old as our species, human sexual behavior. Billions of humans were sexual creatures. Nonetheless, the subject was taboo in the Puritanical America that surrounded Kinsey. But, fortunately for us, nothing human was alien to Dr. Kinsey. He wanted to know the facts, the whole truth and nothing but the truth, about sex. He sought to shine light in a sexual age filled with dark misconceptions.

Kinsey took a revolutionary step forward. He invited men and women volunteers to visit his office and discuss when, how often, what kind of, and with whom, they had sex. Over the years, Kinsey personally interviewed 8,000 individuals, including writers Cornelia Otis Skinner and Katherine Anne Porter, and his Bloomington associates added 10,000 more. These 18,000 persons responded to upwards of 521 confidential questions. From this massive data, Kinsey discovered shocking truths. He found, for example, that 13% of the male population was predominantly homosexual. This fact convinced Kinsey that to imprison males for "deviant behavior" (homosexuality) was both impractical and unjust.

In 1948, Kinsey's landmark SEXUAL BEHAVIOR IN THE HUMAN MALE was published. It sold a phenomenal 200,000 hardbound copies in the first two months. His SEXUAL BEHAVIOR IN THE HUMAN FEMALE, published in 1953, was also well received. These books made an enormous contribution to society. They opened the door to more rational, healthy attitudes about sex. His publications created a more agreeable reality. Kinsey's advance occurred because he (and later investigators such as Masters and Johnson) scientifically studied the world as it is, rather than the world as ideologues would have it.

Powerful persons look beyond dogmatism. Many humans arrogantly assert their opinions. It is easy to find New Yorkers who swear that all doberman pinschers are vicious, man-eating dogs and Moscovites who curse that all stockbrokers are avaricious, child-beating monsters. Most of these New Yorkers and Moscovites never think to test their convictions. If you introduce them to a friendly doberman or stockbroker, their rigid dogma is unaffected. Successful persons are flexible. They observe, record, and evaluate their doctrines. If their preconceptions are correct, they keep them. If their beliefs are wrong, they find better ones. Persons who will not face reality are bigots; those who cannot are fools; and those who dare not are slaves. Power-seekers will, can, and dare confront reality.

The fusion of theory and practice is the eighth ingredient of power. Most persons are specialists. In particular, they tend to focus upon either concepts or deeds. There are botanists who know much about stomata, small openings which control leaves' exchanges of gases and water vapor with the atmosphere, but who cannot prune roses. Similarly, there are gardeners who harvest splendid orchids but who cannot classify Angiosperms. Sometimes this division of humanity causes bad feelings exemplified by lawyers who deride "stupid" car mechanics and street sweepers who in turn mock "sissy" school teachers. Power-seekers must look beyond these petty, self-destructive ego games. Every successful venture oscillates between imagination and perspiration. To act takes strength and courage; to think takes intelligence and discipline. Power results when we act according to our thoughts.

The common split between speech and action has at least two origins. The first is historical. Ancient Greece, like many cultures before and after it, was built on the backs of forgotten slaves. Immortal Greeks, such as Plato and Aristotle, supported this slavery. These sages believed that the mind was superior to the body and that worthwhile citizens were those who had ample leisure time to speculate about the universe. Slaves and manual laborers were judged beasts of burden with muscles but no brains. Over the centuries, this worldview has prevailed. Nobility has spent time cultivating wit, while serfs have devoted their lives plowing dirt. Our industrial society, which encourages theoretical physicists to feel superior to applied physicists, shares this longstanding bias. Consequently, many persons welcome sterile rhetoric and shun pregnant labor.

Bertrand Russell noted that, if he had sufficient funds to pay an army, he could convince the public that $2 + 2 = 5$ on sacred holidays and $2 + 2 = 4$ on all other days. The British philosopher realized an important truth. Most people's ideas come from their leaders, whereas most individuals' behavior grows out of their personal experience. This split cause much human suffering.

Nowhere is this more explicit than in politics. Arkady N. Shevchenko, who was the ranking Russian at the United Nations before he defected to the United States in 1978, turned against Russia because he tired of ideology that was irrelevant to daily Soviet life. After Shevchenko escaped to the West, his wife was taken back back to

Russia and, allegedly, committed suicide.

Less dramatic turmoil occurs all around us. Psychiatrists' couches (and many living room sofas) are crowded with tormented adults who cannot resolve their belief that sex is sinful with their experience that sex is enjoyable. And society is full of persons who intellectually want to make friends and to stop gambling but who habitually dodge strangers and follow horse races.

The gap between words and feats is inconsistency, hypocrisy, or confusion, depending upon our generosity. But, more importantly, this disunion is debilitating. Power-seekers cannot afford to work against themselves. As Goethe noted, all truly wise thoughts have been thought thousands of times; but to make them truly ours, we must think them over again honestly, until they take root in our personal experience. To optimize power, individuals' opinions, emotions, and motions must be coordinated into one unified force. Thought, in order to justify itself, must lead to action.

History offers us many unified individuals. These persons, for all their human faults, were uncommonly able to blend abstract concepts and concrete realities. Henry Ford is often viewed as a no-nonsense businessman, what Americans fondly call a "man of action." But Ford, who said, "Thinking is the hardest work there is, which is the probable reason why so few engage in it," had a revolutionary vision that mass production was possible. He succeeded, for better or worse, to transform this notion into assembly lines. Thomas Jefferson, considered by many of his contemporaries to be overly intellectual, transformed the writings of d'Alembert, Rousseau, and Montesquieu into the very practical American Declaration of Independence. This Jeffersonian document supported

George Washington, Simon Bolivar, and other world leaders to create radically new political orders.

Reciprocity is the ninth ingredient of power. Many ambitious persons are surly. They take a low view of human character and assess society as a hostile rat race. Blinded by cynicism, they are takers. They say hello to you, if and only if you can benefit them in the short-term. Many writers deplore that their readers do not mail them fan letters, just as salespersons grumble that their clients do not refer new customers. But it rarely occurs to these complainers that, if they congratulated their favorite authors and promoted their best buyers, their energy would be returned in kind. Their success is limited by their inability to visualize life as a two-way street.

Cooperation, not rivalry, is the foundation of success. In the 18th century, Mayer Anselm Rothschild began loaning money from his home in a Frankfurt, Germany ghetto. His one-man bank was expanded by his five sons. One son stayed in Frankfurt, while the others moved to Vienna, London, Naples, and Paris, where they opened branch offices. The elder Rothschild gave his sons to major rules: first, share all operations with each other and, secondly, never aim at exorbitant profits. Sharing within the family is obvious reciprocity. But so was the patriarch's second maxim. Anselm recognized that outrageous profits would destroy both his clients and his family. He sensed that agreements, be they between individuals or governments, are honored only if all parties benefit from the continuing relationship. The rest is history. The Rothschilds became Europe's most outstanding business family. By comparison, countless five-son families around the globe destroy themselves with infighting, divorces, and law suits, all because they place competition above cooperation.

The best way to help yourself is to aid others. This is one of life's deepest ironies. John Archibald Wheeler is an eminent physicist who, among many other contributions, helped explain astronomical black holes. Professor Wheeler is, also, one of the world's premier teachers. Several of his former students have earned the Nobel Prize. One reason for Wheeler's prominence is his generosity. At scientific conferences, many speakers take undue credit for theories and experimental data that, in reality, belongs to their students and assistants. Wheeler is an exception to the rule. He publicly praises his younger colleagues and lets them report their findings to the scientific community. In turn, Wheeler's grateful students aid his reputation throughout their long careers.

Human responsiveness is vital to success. Suppose a citizens' group is angered by excessive medical costs and is determined to voice their opinion. If they mail an articulate letter to a cross-section of individuals, it is almost certain that United States Senators, insurance company presidents, and hospital directors will answer them more earnestly than low-level bureaucrats. The bureaucrats have a narrow vision. They cannot see the connection between their future and the strangers' protests. Consequently, these paper-shufflers are likely to toss the letter in a waste basket. Intelligent leaders know that they must find a common ground with the public in order to prosper. For their own survival, they take the letter and its authors seriously.

People treat themselves the same way they act towards others. Power-seekers genuinely hunger to climb upward. The best way to accomplish this ascent is self-respect at every step. This esteem requires empathy, the ability to reciprocate with persons less advanced, equal to, and more advanced than themselves. Weak persons boast that they step on inferiors and con superiors. In fact, they are are stepping on and conning themselves. Power-seekers do not underestimate themselves, or anyone else. Rather, they practice the Affirmist Rule: Affirm the best in others, as you would have others affirm the best in you. The most powerful persons are those who reciprocate at the highest levels.

Relaxation is the tenth, and last, ingredient of power. Many ambitious persons are overly competitive, impatient, and angry. They take their hearts, which beat five thousand times an hour and more than three billion times in a life-time of eighty years, and their whole bodies for granted. They keep absorbing more and more stress until, one day, they suffer a stroke, endure a heart attack, or cross the line into mental illness. These sad workaholics are slaves, not masters. Wise power-seekers realize that humans are biological systems that need periodic leisure. They agree with Plutarch, the Greek biographer, that rest is the sweet sauce of labor. They sail boats, plant apple trees, admire Renoir paintings, or otherwise take a break from life's battles. They unwind and recuperate in order to prevent breakdowns and to recharge their batteries.

Periods of reduced tension put life into perspective. All persons, even the most creative ones, are blinded by routine and habit. Picasso would never have generated so many artistic phases, if he had spent every minute painting. Wine, women, and song added much to his work. An American Indian tribe taught that, after every tenth step, persons should stop and look where they have come from and where they are going. Powerful persons, who travel so far from childhood to maturity, especially need to pause and reset their internal compass. Often, the most stubborn problems seem trivial while listening to Bach, reading Mark Twain, or hiking Swiss Alps. These activities make humans more flexible and open windows to opportunity. Those who make good use of life allow valuable space for recreation.

Relaxation is enjoyable. It feels good to breathe pine scented air and to swim in the moonlight as if the moment was eternal. Life is short and, without pleasure and exuberance, it is a dreary ordeal. We have come full circle. In the beginning, we said that humans are born to seek power. We hunger for power, as we hunger for seafood or a thousand other delights, because we affirm that power is more joyful than weakness.

FURTHER READING

Aristotle. THE POLITICS. Translated by T.A. Sinclair. Middlesex, England: Penguin Classics, 1979.

Bacard, Andre. AFFIRMIST MANIFESTO. Stanford, California: Modern Studies Group, 1982.

Bacard, Andre. 'Power, Impotence, and the Individual.' Stanford, California: Modern Studies Group, 1980.

Bateson, Gregory. MIND AND NATURE: A NECESSARY UNITY. New York: Dutton, 1979.

Berger, John. SUCCESS AND FAILURE OF PICASSO. Middlesex, England: Penguin Books, 1965.

Bronowski, Jacob. THE ASCENT OF MAN. Boston: Little, Brown, 1973.

Bugliosi, Vincent. HELTER SKELTER. New York, Bantam, 1975.

Carlyle, Thomas. ON HEROES, HERO-WORSHIP, AND THE HEROIC IN HISTORY. Edited by Archibald MacMechan. Boston: Atheneum Press, 1901.

Caro, Robert A. THE POWER BROKER. New York: Knopf, 1974.

Castaneda, Carlos. THE TEACHINGS OF DON JUAN. New York: Ballantine, 1968.

Chomsky, Noam. AMERICAN POWER AND THE NEW MANDARINS. New York: Pantheon, 1969.

Clark, Ronald. EINSTEIN: THE LIFE AND TIMES. New York: World Pub. Co., 1971.

de Tocqueville, Alexis. DEMOCRACY IN AMERICA. Translated by George Lawrence. New York: Harper & Row, 1966.

Dobrovir, William A. and others. THE OFFENSES OF RICHARD M. NIXON. New York: Quadrangle, 1973.

Domhoff, G. William. THE BOHEMIAN GROVE AND OTHER RETREATS. New York: Harper & Row, 1975.

Durant, Will. THE STORY OF CIVILIZATION. Ten volume series. New York: Simon & Schuster, 1935-1967.

Durant, Will and Ariel. THE LESSONS OF HISTORY. New York: Simon & Schuster, 1968.

Feynman, Richard P. 'SURELY YOU'RE JOKING, MR. FEYNMAN!': ADVENTURES OF A CURIOUS CHARACTER. New York: W. W. Norton, 1985.

Fowles, John. THE COLLECTOR. New York: Dell Publishing Company, 1975.

Fowles, John. THE MAGUS. Boston: Little, Brown, 1965.

Freud, Sigmund. CIVILIZATION AND ITS DISCONTENTS. Translated by James Strachey. New York: W.W. Norton, 1962.

Fromm, Erich. ESCAPE FROM FREEDOM. New York: Holt, Rinehart, and Wilson, 1972.

Fromm, Erich. THE ART OF LOVING. New York: Harper, 1956.

Galbraith, John Kenneth. THE ANATOMY OF POWER. Boston: Houghton Mifflin, 1983.

Gross, Ronald. THE INDEPENDENT SCHOLAR'S HANDBOOK. Reading, Massachusetts: Addison-Wesley, 1982.

Haley, J. Evetts. A TEXAN LOOKS AT LYNDON. Canyon, Texas: Palo Duro Press, 1964.

Hersh, Seymour. PRICE OF POWER: KISSINGER IN THE NIXON WHITE HOUSE. New York: Summit Books, 1983.

Hook, Sidney. THE HERO IN HISTORY. London: Secker & Warburg, 1945.

Ludwig, Emil. GENIUS AND CHARACTER. Translated by Kenneth Burke. New York: Harcourt, Brace & Company, 1928.

Kautsky, Karl. FOUNDATIONS OF CHRISTIANITY. Translated by Jacob W. Hartmann. New York: Monthly Review Press, 1972.

Kolenda, Konstantin. PHILOSOPHY IN LITERATURE: METAPHYSICAL DARKNESS AND ETHICAL LIGHT. Totowa, N.J.: Barnes & Noble, 1982.

Korda, Michael. POWER! New York: Random House, 1975.

Kurtz, Paul. EXUBERANCE. Buffalo, New York: Prometheus Books, 1977.

Lamont, Corliss. THE PHILOSOPHY OF HUMANISM. New York: Ungar, 1982.

May, Rollo. POWER AND INNOCENCE. New York: Norton, 1972.

Machiavelli, Niccolo. THE PRINCE. Introduction by Christian Gauss. New York: New American Library, 1964.

Mao, Tse-Tung. QUOTATIONS FROM CHAIRMAN MAO TSE-TUNG. Peking, China: Foreign Languages Press, 1967.

Michaud, Stephen G. THE ONLY LIVING WITNESS. New York: Simon & Schuster, 1983.

Milgram, Stanley. OBEDIENCE TO AUTHORITY. New York: Harper & Row, 1974.

Mills, Jeannie. SIX YEARS WITH GOD: LIFE INSIDE REV. JIM JONES'S PEOPLE'S TEMPLE. New York: A & W Publishers, 1979.

Nietzsche, Friedrich. THE WILL TO POWER. Translated by Walter Kaufmann and R.J. Hollingdale. Edited by Walter Kaufmann. New York: Random House, 1968.

Nietzsche, Friedrich. THUS SPOKE ZARATHUSTRA. Translated by R.J. Hollingdale. Middlesex, England: Penguin Classics, 1969.

Ortega Y Gasset, Jose. THE REVOLT OF THE MASSES. London: George Allen & Unwin, 1963.

Orwell, George. 1984. New York: New American Library, 1983.

Paine, Thomas. RIGHTS OF MAN. New York: Heritage Press, 1961.

Pauling, Linus. NO MORE WAR! New York: Dodd, Mead & Co, 1983.

Rand, Ayn. THE FOUNTAINHEAD. Indianapolis, In-dianapolis, Indiana: Bobbs-Merrill Company, 1943.

Rawls, John. A THEORY OF JUSTICE. Cambridge, Massachusetts: Harvard Press, 1971.

Rodgers, Carl. ON PERSONAL POWER. New York: Delacorte Press, 1977.

Rougier, Louis. 'Philosophical Origins of the Idea of Natural Equality.' MODERN AGE. 18 (WINTER 1974).

Rothschild, Guy de. THE WHIMS OF FORTUNE. New York: Random House, 1985.

Russell, Bertrand. AUTHORITY AND THE IN-
DIVIDUAL. New York: AMS Press, 1949.

Russell, Bertrand. POWER. New York: W.W. Norton &
Company, 1969.

Russell, Bertrand. UNPOPULAR ESSAYS. New York:
Simon & Schuster, 1945.

Sagan, Carl. COSMOS. New York: Random House, 1983.

Schild, Alfred. 'On the Matter of Freedom.' Austin:
Texas: THE GRADUATE JOURNAL (of the University of Texas), Fall 1959.

Solzhenitsyn, Alexander. 'The Exhausted West.' HAR-
VARD MAGAZINE, July-August 1978.

Stern, Philip M. THE OPPENHEIMER CASE. New York,
Harper & Row, 1969.

Streiker, Lowell D. THE GOSPEL TIME BOMB. Buffalo,
New York: Prometheus Books, 1984.

Suetonius. THE TWELVE CAESARS. Translated by
Robert Graves. Middlesex, England: Penguin
Classics, 1970.

Wilson, Colin. A CRIMINAL HISTORY OF MANKIND.
New York: G.P. Putnam's, 1984.

INDEX

FOR FURTHER INFORMATION

If you want to order additional copies of **HUNGER FOR POWER,** contact Andre Bacard, or be on Heroica's mailing list, write:

Heroica Books
Box 12718-A, Northgate Station
San Rafael, California 94913, USA